Eureka!

Science Demonstrations for ESL Classes

Stephen Gomez

Heather McKay

Abigail Tom

Kathleen White

Addison-Wesley Publishing Company

Reading, Massachusetts • Menlo Park, California • New York • Don Mills, Ontario
Wokingham, England, • Amsterdam • Bonn • Sydney • Singapore • Tokyo
Madrid • San Juan • Paris • Seoul • Milan • Mexico City • Taipei, Taiwan

A Publication of the World Language Division

Editorial: Clare Siska and Talbot Hamlin
Production: Kathy Sands Boehmer
Interior Design: Michelle Taverniti
Illustrations: Kathleen White
Cover Design: Marshall Henrichs
Manufacturing: James W. Gibbons

ISBN: 0-201-59508-7
1 2 3 4 5 6 7 8 9 10–CRS–98 97 96 95

See page 186 for a list of pages that may be reproduced for classroom use.

To our students, who have taught us so much

CONTENTS

INTRODUCTION

For many years, language teachers worked on the assumption that language teaching was a separate entity from content teaching. It is now clear that the two cannot take place effectively in isolation from each other. Language learned in isolation is meaningless. By teaching language and content together, we give meaning and interest to language learning and provide students with academically useful knowledge and skills.

In this book, the content is science. Because it lends itself to graphic demonstrations and explanations, science can be taught to students within a wide range of English proficiency. Furthermore, science is not culturally dependent in the same way that history and literature are. All students, regardless of their educational backgrounds, come with some basic observations and knowledge about science. It is, therefore, a subject in which students' previous knowledge, as well as their natural curiosity, can be recognized and built upon. The hands-on lessons in this book are designed to draw on these student characteristics.

In addition, through these lessons, students become familiar with basic principles of science. They also learn to predict, to observe, to record their observations, and to report on what they have seen—essential skills in science and in other areas. These experiences facilitate success in regular academic classes.

ESL students are happy to find that they can learn "real" subject matter while they are learning English. They have authentic reasons to use English as they predict, participate in, and read about their experience. They become invested in learning through their participation. They are able to succeed in learning. Best of all, they have fun.

The beginning and focal point for each lesson is the presentation of a short, easily executed science demonstration. These demonstrations have been selected because they are attention getting and provocative, stimulating talk and curiosity. Another basis for selection is that they are easy to do and require no special equipment or space. The materials used in each one, such as straws, balloons, and string, are inexpensive and easily obtained. Detailed directions and explanations guide the teacher through each demonstration. Little prior knowledge of science on the teacher's part is assumed. Each demonstration is accompanied by activities designed to expand students' knowledge of English as well as of science.

The lessons are organized into the following units: Introduction to Scientific Processes, Properties of Air, Force and Motion, Electricity and Magnetism, Visual Perception, Sound, Properties of Liquids, Chemistry, and Heat. With a few exceptions, each lesson is a separate entity and can be used by itself. The age and interests of your students, as well as your curriculum, will help you decide which ones to use.

The Notes to the Teacher, which follow this Introduction, provide many specific suggestions for using the lessons. We hope they will guide you in getting the most out of *Eureka!*

NOTES TO THE TEACHER

Selecting Lessons • We do not intend for teachers to follow this book from beginning to end, although in a few cases we have suggested a sequence of related lessons. Instead, you should select those that relate to your other classroom activities and that are compatible with your local school and community setting. Table 1 (page 181) correlates common ESL themes with lessons to suggest where each lesson might fit.

As examples of lessons that relate to other classroom activities, Lesson 14, Balloon Rockets, might be part of a study of transportation. Lessons from the Visual Perception and Sound units fit well with work on the human body. We once did Lesson 50, Will It or Won't It?, in response to student questions in a polar lands unit about how large animals, such as polar bears, are able to float.

In selecting lessons, you also need to take into account which demonstrations and activities are feasible in your classroom and which you think you and your students would enjoy. We hope that the pictures, done by Kathleen White, one of the authors, will help you in choosing lessons. These pictures are deliberately simple so that teachers or students can readily copy them on the board, on a transparency, or in a notebook.

Some of the demonstrations are intended to be done by the teacher and a few student volunteers, and others by all of the students. We have based our recommendations on several factors: safety, cost or complexity of materials, classroom control, and the element of surprise. However, class size, facilities, and age of students may enter into your decision about whether to have the entire class or only a few students take an active part.

The first unit, Introduction to Scientific Processes, is designed to acquaint students with some of the skills they need in science as well as in many other academic fields. These include classifying, observing, predicting, inferring, hypothesizing, interpreting data, and measuring. These same skills recur throughout the book. However, because the focus is on the skills themselves, the lessons do not include the Application and Explanation sections found in the later lessons.

Organization of the Lessons • Each lesson, with the exception of those in the first unit as noted above, follows the same format. Most begin with a simple picture that will help you select and set up the demonstration. This picture can be photocopied or drawn by you or a student and used as an introduction to or a review of a lesson.

Each lesson includes a list of materials needed. It is important to check this list ahead of time so that you have everything ready to complete the demonstration. We have tried throughout this book to limit demonstrations to those requiring materials that are found around the house or that are easily purchased. Balloons, drinking straws, fishing line, string, coins, and tape are among these items. A few of the materials may be a bit harder to find, in which case we have included suggestions about finding them.

The next section of each lesson is the Demonstration: a series of step-by-step directions. Before beginning a demonstration, read through the steps and decide how you want to present it. Consider ways to provide language input as well as ways to elicit students' previous knowledge and ideas. As a start, you may want to look over the suggestions in "Getting the Most Language Out of Each Lesson," below.

In the Analysis section, students are actively involved in trying to solve the puzzle posed by the demonstration. In this stage, students describe and share their observations in a variety of ways, including reports, discussions, further observation, asking and answering questions, directed speculation, charts, graphs, drawings, or models.

The next section is the Application. In this section, students are encouraged to actively explore the "so what?" of the demonstration, to make links between their new knowledge and other events in the world around them. This takes several forms, including pictures, stories, and activities.

The Explanation appears after the Application section, but you will probably want to use this information between the Analysis and the Application steps. The explanation is intended, first of all, to provide you, the teacher, with an understanding of what takes place in the demonstration. You can then use this information in a variety of ways. You may want to explain what happened in your own words as you sketch the demonstration. You may want to elicit an explanation from your students. For more advanced students, you may prefer to use the explanations just as they are written for listening or reading practice.

Some lessons also include Follow-up activities for further enhancing students' exploration and understanding of the topic.

Reproducible student pages are provided for some demonstrations as well as for some analysis and application activities and for the explanations.

We have not suggested a length of time for each lesson, because how long you spend on a given lesson really depends on you. You may want to complete the entire lesson in one class period, or you may want to divide it over parts of two or more class periods. The latter has the advantage of providing more opportunity for reviewing and retelling what has happened.

Getting the Most Language Out of Each Lesson • It is important to exploit the language-learning potential in each lesson. Here we present a number of suggestions for doing so. Rather than including vocabulary as a separate section in each lesson, words that are likely to be new to the students are identified in bold print and can be found in the Glossary which appears in the back of this book. In many instances, words are defined in the Explanation. The Demonstration provides a meaningful context in which to introduce and practice these words. Suggestions for working with vocabulary are included here and in the demonstrations themselves.

A number of grammatical/structural items recur throughout the lessons, generated by the activities themselves. Table 2 (page 184) correlates these items with the different steps of the demonstrations and will help you to be aware of them as you use the materials. Activities designed to get the most language out of each step of the demonstrations are enumerated on the Table and expanded upon here.

Pictures. For lessons that include pictures, show the students the picture or copy it on the board or on an overhead before the demonstration. Have students guess what will happen. The picture can then be used to introduce new vocabulary. You can ask students to set up the demonstration after looking at the picture or, alternatively, you (or a student partner) can describe the picture, and the students or partner can set up the demonstration based on what they hear. Students can be asked to draw and label the picture. All or some of the labels can be dictated or, for beginning students, the labels may simply be copied. Each student can be given a partially labeled copy of the picture. Partners would then fill in the missing labels from information given by the other partner. Students can simply be shown the picture with no explanation except what they can elicit through their own questions. Note: Some lessons do not include pictures.

After the demonstration (on the same or the following day), you or one or more students can draw the picture on a transparency or on the board. Class members can give directions for the drawing. Individuals can make and label drawings. These post-demonstration activities provide students with an opportunity to review the demonstration and the new vocabulary. They also give a student who has been absent a chance to catch up on missed work. The drawing can also be used as a basis for written work with students writing a description of their drawing either before or after the demonstration.

Materials. You can keep what you need for a given lesson in a shoe box and bring it out a piece at a time in order to keep students' attention focused—and to increase their suspense. Build in opportunities for students to participate. As you bring out each piece, have the students name and describe it and try to predict how all the pieces will be used together. Encourage the students to ask questions about the equipment. If you are setting up the demonstration in front of the class, keep up a running commentary telling what you are doing. Ask students questions as you set up the demonstration. (For example, ask *Do you like 7-Up?* while pouring it during the demonstration of Lesson 53, Bubble Babies. Follow up with the question, *What do you think we'll be using this for?*)

Demonstration. If students are doing the demonstrations themselves, the instructions may be given in oral or written form. They can be dictated to students; you can have students read them; or you can post the instructions and have a "runner" from each group read and transfer them to the other group members. Encourage the students to seek clarification of the directions and to talk to one another about what is happening.

Analysis. We have indicated in each lesson a specific technique for analysis. These include answering questions and summarizing. Some involve *channel conversion*—converting information received in one form (orally or through observation) into another (making charts, drawing pictures). Student retellings of their observations can be transcribed and used for language experience work. Many of the Analysis activities require students to solve problems.

Application. The applications take a number of forms, such as stories, examples of everyday occurrences illustrating the demonstration, and additional experiments the students can do. The applications serve to link the demonstrations to other classroom topics, such as weather, geography, or food. Students should be encouraged to make these links verbally, using ideas and vocabulary from the lessons as well as from their other class work.

Explanation. A great deal of language can be elicited by having the students themselves explain what they think happened in the demonstration. Your role in this is to encourage and direct speculation by asking questions. You can give the explanation orally or have a student informant do so. The written explanation, phrased in language that an intermediate to advanced student can understand, is printed at the end of each lesson. If you choose to do so, you can make a photocopy of the explanation and hand it out to the class. It can be used, as any text for this level can, in a variety of ways. For example, it could be a jigsaw reading, with different group members having access to different parts. After reading their separate parts, the students pool the information they each have. One or two group members could have access to the text and explain or dictate it to the rest. One way to do this is by having a kind of relay race, with one student reading the text and giving the information to a "runner," who passes the information on to a "writer" situated at the other end of the room. The text can be cut up for group members to assemble. It can be rewritten as a cloze passage. The text can be put on an overhead and revealed a bit at a time. Students can rewrite an explanation for a different audience, such as their younger brothers and sisters. Finally, you can present the text orally as a partial dictation, with students filling in missing words as they listen.

On Doing the Demonstrations • The following suggestions will help you make the most of the demonstrations in your classroom.

1. Try the demonstration yourself first to be sure it will go smoothly. Don't do this in front of the students or it will spoil the surprise.

2. Be sure to have all the equipment at hand and ready to use.

3. Make adaptations as needed for your particular students. Include various levels of questions and commentary. For beginning students, questions or requests requiring nonverbal responses are appropriate. (*Who likes grapes? Which is the empty glass? Pull the string tight.*) More advanced students are expected to participate more actively in questioning and speculating as well as summarizing what they have learned. In the demonstrations, roles requiring a minimal production of language can be found for beginners so that they are active participants in the activity. More advanced students might be asked to read and explain directions. In a bilingual class, parts of the lesson can be done in L1 and others in L2.

Introduction to Scientific Processes

I. MYSTERY BOX

Skills • Observation, prediction, inference

Materials • One mystery box (about the size of a stationery box) for each group of three students. In each box put a different kind of object or objects which will make a noise when rolled around, such as marbles, dowels, blocks, a roll of masking tape, toothpicks, rice, pencils. Put the top on each box and tape it shut. Write a number on the outside of each box. One Mystery Box Observation Sheet for each group.

Demonstration

1. Hold up a mystery box and ask the students if they have ever gotten a present and tried to discover what was inside. What kinds of things did they do to the box to get clues about its contents?

2. Tell the students that each group will have a turn at trying to find out the contents of each box. They may shake the box, turn it at different angles, hold it to see how heavy it is, smell it and do anything else that will help them determine the contents except open the box. All boxes must remain sealed. The members of each group will work together to try to guess the contents of each box.

3. Pass out the Mystery Box Observation Sheets and tell the students to record their observations on it. Look at the various categories with them and show them the lines where they can add their own descriptors.

4. Hand out a box to each group. After two or three minutes, tell the students to record their observations and guesses. Then each group will pass its box on to another group and begin the process again.

5. When each group has had a chance to guess at all the boxes, tell them to keep the last box. Have the groups take turns stating their guesses for one box at a time. After each group guesses the contents of a box, have the students holding that box open it and show the contents.

Analysis • Ask the students to compare the strategies they used to make their guesses. Did most of the groups use the same strategies? Were any different?

Follow-up • Let each group make a mystery box for the other groups and repeat the guessing process. If time permits, partner boxes can also be made. For each student you will need a small box with a lid (film canisters, jewelry boxes, etc. can be used), contents for each box such as rice, coins, toothpicks, pushpins, paper clips, pencil erasers, thumbtacks, small wooden cubes, rubber bands, washers, screws. Each box must have a partner box filled with identical items. Have the students walk around the room, comparing the sounds of their boxes and looking for the partner box which makes the same sound. When partners find each other, they must sit down. When all partners have been matched, have each pair open their boxes and compare the contents. This is a good "get acquainted" activity.

• MYSTERY BOX •

Fill in the number of each box as you examine it. Put a check in the box beside the word or words that describe the clues you get from the box. In the blank spaces at the bottom of the chart, add other words you need.

Box Numbers

Describing Words									
rattle									
roll									
slide									
heavy									
light									
more than 1									
clank									
small pieces									

2. PAPER CHANGE

Skills • Observation, conducting an experiment, prediction

Materials • One 4" × 6" index card, a ruler, and a pair of scissors for each student.

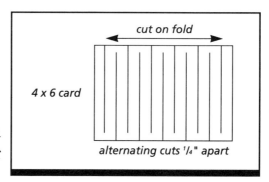

Demonstration

1. Pass out the index cards. Have the students tell you about them: size, shape, material. Ask them if the card is big enough to fit around their heads. Tell them that they are going to change the shape of the cards so that they will be able to put them around their heads.

2. Give the directions orally, and demonstrate as you do so. First have them fold the card in half lengthwise. Pass out the rulers. Help the students locate ¼ inch on them. Then have them start at one end of the card and mark ¼ inch intervals.

3. With the scissors, make a cut ¼ inch from one end, beginning from the folded side. The cut should go to ¼ inch from the other side of the card. Then make similar cuts, alternating sides, at ¼ inch intervals to the other end of the card, ending with a cut from the folded side. In each case, the cut should end ¼ inch from the edge.

4. Put the point of the scissors under the fold after the first cut. Cut the fold except for the first and last ¼ inch.

5. Open the card. How big is it? Will it fit over your head?

Analysis • Ask the students to consider these questions: *How has the card changed? Is it the same size it was before? Did cutting it make it bigger or smaller? Is the whole card still there?*

3. OUTDOOR SCAVENGER HUNT

Skills • Observation, classification

Materials • One large manila envelope for every three students, one copy of the Outdoor Scavenger Hunt List for each group, newspaper to cover tables, butcher paper, markers, and glue for graph.

Demonstration

1. Show the students an empty soda can and a rock. Ask them to tell some ways the two objects are different. If no one says "made by nature" and "made by people," suggest it yourself. Have the students name some other things which belong in each category.

2. Tell the students that you are all going outside to look for things that are made by people and things that are natural. Divide the class into groups of three. Hand out and go over the list of items. Be sure the students understand the meaning of each category. Before going outside, you can ask the students to generate further categories of things they might expect to find. Alternatively, they can add more categories as they come across them. As they find items, they are to list them under the appropriate category. Pass out the envelopes.

3. Go outside with the students. Give them fifteen minutes to collect the items. Caution the students not to destroy or damage plants.

4. When you return to the classroom, have the students dump the contents of their envelopes on the paper-covered desks. Ask the groups to share interesting or unusual items.

5. Ask the students to think of a way they could divide their items into four groups. Call on each group to explain how they did it. Repeat this classification activity one or two more times, asking the students to think of other ways to divide the items.

6. Have the students divide their items into the two groups you discussed earlier: made by nature and made by people. Which

group was larger? Which items were easier to find? Have the students make inferences about and discuss human influence on their environment.

Analysis • Have the students work together to make a graph on a large sheet of butcher paper using the items they found outside. They should label one line on the paper *natural* and the other *manmade*, leaving enough space between the lines so that items can be glued on the graph. Have each group take turns gluing their items side by side on the graph. Allow the graph to dry overnight before hanging it up.

Follow-up • Students might be interested in starting a schoolwide clean-up or recycling project after this activity.

OUTDOOR
• SCAVENGER HUNT LIST •

Find and describe the following items:

1. Unusual rock_____

2. Evidence of an animal _____

3. A seed _____

4. Evidence of people_____

5. Something smooth _____

6. Something rough _____

7. A shell _____

8. Something green _____

9. Something that smells _____

10. Something that was once alive _____

11. _____

12. _____

13. _____

14. _____

15. _____

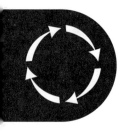

4. ANIMAL TRACKS

Skills • Observation, inference, drawing conclusions

Materials • One copy per student of the Students' Animal Tracks Story and the Animal Tracks and Facts Sheet; one copy of Teacher's Animal Tracks Story (or an overhead transparency of the story).

Demonstration

1. Ask the students to tell you what they know about animal tracks. Encourage them to share their own observations of animal tracks. Tell them that they are going to look at a picture of animal tracks which tells a story. They will be detectives and observe the tracks carefully to find out what happened.

2. Introduce the words *predator* and *prey*, explaining that predators are animals that hunt others, while prey are the animals they hunt. Use examples like coyotes and rabbits or snakes and mice. Have the students suggest other predator/prey relationships.

3. Show the students the Teacher's Animal Tracks Story (on the overhead, if possible). Tell them that the tracks in the picture tell a story. The story happened in a sandy desert. The students are going to be detectives and figure out what happened.

4. Guide the students as they reconstruct the story. Who or what made the tracks in the desert sand? What might have happened? Give the students a few minutes to think about the story. Have students tell their solutions.

5. Pass out copies of the Students' Animal Tracks Story. Tell the students to look at the tracks carefully and identify the animals. Remind them about predators and prey. Have the students write stories about what they think happened. This can be done individually or in pairs.

Analysis • Have the students read their stories. Did they find reasonable solutions based on their observations of the tracks?

Application • Have the students use the Animal Tracks and Facts sheet to make their own footprint stories. Let them share the stories with the rest of the class.

Follow-up • Have students watch for animal tracks when they go home from class. Have them draw the ones they find. What were they?

• ANIMAL TRACKS AND FACTS •

1. Coyote

Similar to dog tracks, coyote tracks have claw marks and follow a straight line. They may appear almost anywhere. Coyotes eat snakes, rabbits, mice and other rodents, lizards, berries, etc.

2. Deer

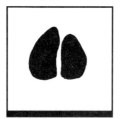

Deer walk on hooves. They are commonly found in forests and brushy areas. They eat plants during the early morning and late evening.

3. Bobcat

Their footprints show two-lobed pads and no claw marks. When they walk, their back feet step in their front footprints. They prefer rocky places. They hunt chipmunks, squirrels, rabbits, and insects at night.

4. Fox

Their footprints have claw marks and hair impressions. They prefer forests. They change diet with the season, eating rodents, berries, and insects.

5. Raccoon

Their tracks look like tiny handprints. They live inside tree holes and are active at night. They feed on fish, grasshoppers, bird eggs, berries—almost anything.

6. Opossum

On their tracks, notice that the inner toes of their back feet look like thumbprints. They move slowly. They eat almost anything: eggs, birds, garbage. They live in woods and near water.

7. Black bear

Their large footprints are easy to identify. They live in the mountains. During the winter, they hibernate and wake up from time to time. They eat berries, insect larvae, squirrels, gophers.

8. Rabbit

They are often found under brush. They feed on green plants and twigs.

9. Robin

Their tracks are in pairs, which indicates that they hop on the ground. They eat worms and insects.

10. Ground beetle

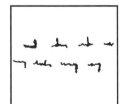

These are found under stones and at the edge of water. They eat caterpillars, other insects, and snails.

11. Roadrunner

Roadrunners live in the desert. They like to eat insects, snakes, and lizards.

12. Kangaroo rat

They live in the desert. They eat seeds.

13. Sidewinder snake

They live in the desert and eat small rodents and lizards.

TEACHER'S
• ANIMAL TRACKS STORY •

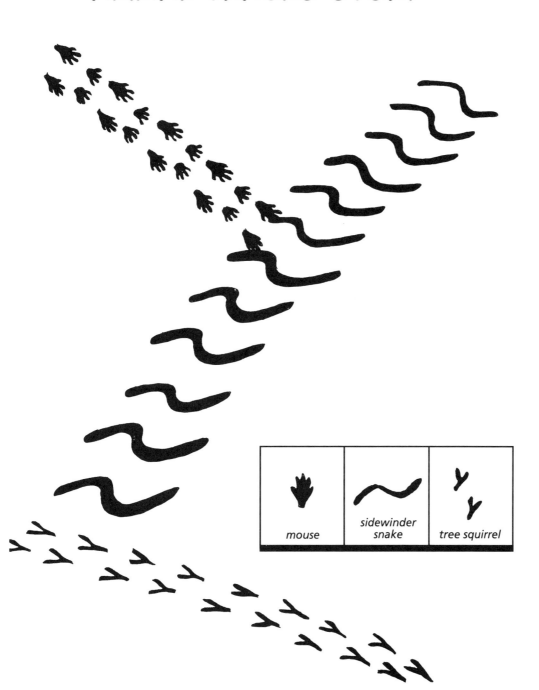

 mouse	 sidewinder snake	 tree squirrel

STUDENTS'
• ANIMAL TRACKS STORY •

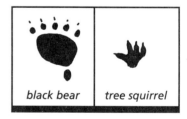

black bear | tree squirrel

5. VARIABLE PARACHUTES

Skills • Controlling variables, observation, conducting an experiment

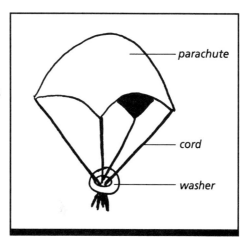

Materials • Pieces of paper of various sizes and weights, a roll of aluminum foil; a roll of plastic wrap; rolls or spools of string, thread, yarn, and/or fishing line of various weights; scissors; objects to be dropped (such as clothes pins, small toys). Have an assortment of objects to be dropped, but enough of one kind so that each group can have one if they decide that everyone should drop the same object. Eggs can be used for greater risk and challenge.

Demonstration

1. Make a rough sketch of a parachute on the board. Ask the students to tell you everything they know about it. Put the word *parachute* on the board, as well as other key words in the students' comments. Encourage discussion by asking them how they work and why they are used. As you wind up the discussion, ask them to tell you how many main parts there are to your parachute drawing. On the drawing, put labels (the parachute itself, the rope or cord, the object or person).

2. Tell the students that they are going to have a parachute contest. Before they make their parachutes, they are going to try to think of all the possible ways that each part of the parachute can be different. Give some examples (number of pieces of cord, shape of parachute, hole in parachute). Divide the class into groups of three or four and have them discuss and list as many variables as they can. You may want to have them make their lists on large pieces of paper for easier presentation to the class.

3. Put the whole class back together. Write the word *variables* on the board. Ask the students if they know what it means. If no one does, tell them that they have just been thinking about variables in making a parachute. Ask if anyone can explain variables with that hint. If no one can, tell them that variables are ways that things can be changed or made different. Have each group present their lists of parachute variables.

4. Ask the students if they want to make any rules to limit the variables in the parachute contest. If so, have them work in groups or as a whole class to decide how to make it a fair contest.

5. Divide the class into groups. Put the materials out for the parachutes. Have each group make its parachute. They may want to test them as they go along. Encourage experimentation and testing.

6. Have the contest. If your building has a second floor, the parachutes can be dropped from there. The students may want to have more than one category of judging, such as time and accuracy. Students or teachers from another class can act as judges.

Analysis • Discuss with the students the results of the contest. What did they learn about the parachute variables? Were there other factors besides the parachutes themselves (e.g., wind, bumping into the building, or other parachutes)?

6. THE BLOB

Skills • Predicting, recording data, conducting an experiment, inferring, drawing conclusions

Materials • One box of cornstarch and one cup (or more) of water per 12 students; a mixing bowl and spoon; for each group of two or three students: a hammer or a rock, two paper cups, 20 inches of string, a plastic sandwich bag, an 8-inch piece of waxed paper, newspaper to cover desk, copy of The Blob Experiment Sheet and The Blob Analysis Sheet. A few drops of food coloring can be added to the water for an interesting effect.

Demonstration

1. Before the class begins, mix the cornstarch and water together in a large mixing bowl. Make as much as needed for the class size. You may find as you mix it that you need to add a bit more water. Do so gradually. When the mixture is ready, there will be no separate grains of cornstarch. It will be thick and shiny on top.

2. Tell the students that you found this Blob at school this morning and you are trying to find out what it is. Walk around the room and let the students look at the Blob. Pick some up with the spoon and let it drip back in the bowl as you do so.

3. Put the words solid and liquid on the board. Ask the students to give you some examples of each. Then have them explain how they know if something is a solid or a liquid. List the characteristics they propose. You may want to stimulate their thinking by asking them what the shape of water is, whether water can be picked up in their hands, whether it can be broken, etc. Explain that during the class the students are going to perform some scientific experiments on the Blob to determine if it is a solid or a liquid.

4. Put the students in groups of two or three. Distribute one set of experiment sheets to each group and review the activities. When the students are ready to begin the experiments, pass out the materials, including one half-full cup of the Blob mixture.

Give the students a few minutes to observe the Blob before beginning the experiments.

Analysis • Have the students compare their observations and the results of their experiments with the facts about solids and liquids on the Blob Analysis Sheet.

Application • Write the following list of foods on the board. Divide the students into pairs or threes and ask them to divide the list into liquids and solids. Compare the groups' results.

ice cream	*a banana*	*spaghetti*
soup	*an orange*	*cheese*
cake	*an egg*	*gelatin* (such as Jell-O)
honey	*bread*	*an apple*

*Name*_____

• THE BLOB •

Observations

1. What color is it?_____

2. What does it feel like? _____

3. What shape is it? _____

4. What does it smell like?_____

5. What else do you observe? _____

Experiments

Do these experiments and mark whether the Blob acts more like a solid or a liquid.

	Solid	Liquid
1. Can you see through the Blob?		
2. Poke your finger into the cup of Blob and try to touch the bottom of the cup in one second.		
3. Poke your finger into the cup of Blob and try to touch the bottom in ten seconds.		
4. Put the Blob in the plastic bag. Does it take the shape of the bag or keep the shape of the cup?		
5. Pour the Blob from one cup to the other.		
6. Hold some of the Blob in your hand and drop it on the waxed paper. Does it bounce?		
7. Put the Blob on the waxed paper and hit it with the hammer or rock. Does it shatter?		
8. Try to form the Blob into a ball. Does it hold its shape for five seconds?		

ANALYSIS SHEET

• THE BLOB •

Facts About Solids and Liquids

Solids

1. Do not change shape easily.

2. Do not allow another solid to pass through them easily.

3. Can usually be seen.

4. Have a definite size and shape.

Liquids

1. Change shape easily, taking the shape of their containers.

2. Allow a solid to pass through them easily.

3. May be visible or invisible.

4. Have a definite size.

Use the facts about solids and liquids to check your answers on the Experiment Sheet. Each numbered space in this pie chart refers to a question on the Experiment Sheet. Use colored pencils to fill in each section. Choose a different color to represent solid and liquid.

What do you think? Is the Blob a solid or a liquid?

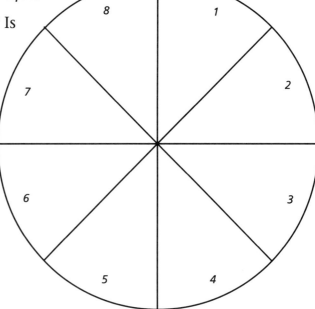

7. INTERLOCKING LOOPS

Skills • Observation, prediction

Materials • For each pair of students: 24-inch strips of paper (cash register tape is ideal), tape, a pencil and a pair of scissors. Alternatively, this can be done as a demonstration by the teacher or one student, in which case you will only need one set of these materials.

Demonstration

1. Hold up one strip of paper and ask the students to tell you how many surfaces the paper has (two) and how many edges (four). Then use a piece of tape to make the paper strip into a circle. Ask them now how many surfaces there are (two) and how many edges (two).

2. Take another strip of paper and twist it once before you join the ends together. Hold up the circular strip and ask the students how many sides it has. Tell them that you want someone to check how many sides the paper has by drawing a line down the middle of each side.

3. Ask a student volunteer to draw a line down the middle of one side without taking the pencil off the paper. Let the students see that the student is able to cover both sides without lifting the pencil. Ask again how many sides the paper circle has.

4. Ask another student volunteer to cut along the line. While she does this, ask the others to predict what will happen. (The result will be one large loop of paper.)

5. Ask another student to cut around this circle to see if the same thing will happen. Again have the other students predict while the volunteer cuts. (This time there will be two interlocked loops.)

6. Have the students repeat steps 2, 3, 4, and 5 in pairs to check the results.

Analysis • Have the students discuss what happened when they repeated the demonstration.

PROPERTIES OF AIR

8. MOVING PAPER

Topic • Air pressure

Materials • A 1" × 6" strip of paper for each pair of students and one for the teacher.

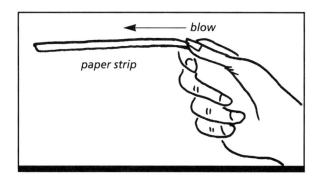

Demonstration

1. Explain to the class that they are going to conduct a scientific experiment using only a strip of paper. Ask them to guess what kind of experiment it might be. Ask the students to predict what will happen if they blow over the strip. Write the predictions on the board.

2. Divide the class into partners and hand out the paper strips.

3. Tell the students to make a 1-inch fold at one end of the paper strip. Demonstrate it as you tell them.

4. Tell them to hold the strip between the thumb and first finger. Then rest the thumb on the chin. Again accompany oral instructions with demonstration.

5. Have both partners take a turn blowing over the paper.

Analysis • Have the students answer the following questions in small groups. *Why did the paper go up when you blew over it? What was different about the air on top of the paper and the air underneath the paper when you blew over it?* Students may want to make a drawing to show their conclusions.

Application • Divide the students into groups and pass out the drawing of an airplane wing. Ask the students to share with the others in their groups what they know about airplanes. What makes them fly? What do their wings look like? Then have them look carefully at the drawing of an airplane wing. Why do they think the wings are designed this way? You may want to write the word **lift** on the board.

Explanation • When you blew over the paper strip, it went up rather than down. By blowing over the top of the paper, you made the air above the strip move faster.

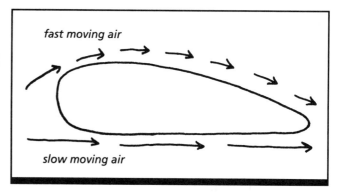

When the air moves faster, the pressure is lower. The higher pressure under the paper lifts it up. This is called **Bernoulli's Principle**.

9. THE UNDERWATER PAPER MYSTERY

Topic • Air occupies space

Materials • A piece of paper, a dry glass or clear plastic cup, a clear plastic container large enough to hold the glass and a person's hand, water, copy of the Underwater Paper Mystery Application Sheet.

Demonstration

1. Introduce the materials to the students. While showing the glass, ask the students to tell you what is in it.

2. Crumple the paper and place it inside the glass, against the bottom. Again ask what is in the glass.

3. Tell the students that you will put the glass with the paper in it under water but that the paper will not get wet. Ask them to guess how this is possible.

4. Fill the large container about three-quarters full of water.

5. Turn the glass over. Be sure the crumpled paper stays in the glass. While holding the glass vertically, open side down, immerse it completely in the water.

6. Remove the glass from the water, still holding it vertically, open side down. Let the water drip off. Then have a student remove the paper from the glass. Pass it around the class so the students can feel that it is not wet.

Analysis • Have the students tell what they saw in the demonstration. As they tell what happened, ask them to try to explain why the paper did not get wet. Were they surprised that the paper did not get wet? What is in the glass besides the paper? What would happen if the glass was put in the water sideways?

Application • With your students, read the paragraph and look at the labeled picture on the application sheet. Discuss the various parts of the picture and how it relates to what they have read.

Explanation • The crumpled paper occupied space in the glass. Besides the paper, there was also air in the glass. When the glass was put in the water, air could not come into the glass because the space was already taken by air. As a result, the paper did not get wet.

• UNDERWATER PAPER •

Everywhere you go, you see bridges, underwater tunnels, and piers. All of these have to be built at least partially under water. To build these structures under water, the work place is enclosed by watertight walls. Then air is pumped into the area, forcing the water out. How does this relate to the demonstration you have just seen?

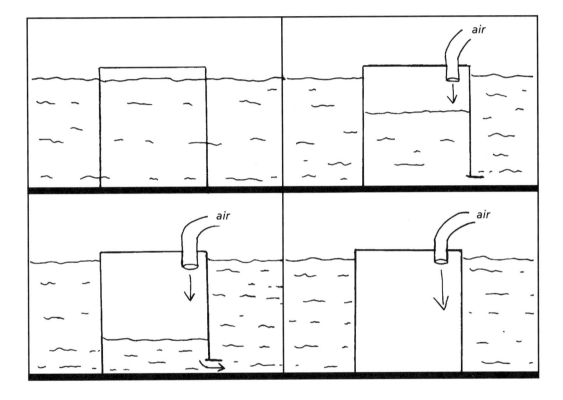

10. THE UPSIDE-DOWN GLASS OF WATER

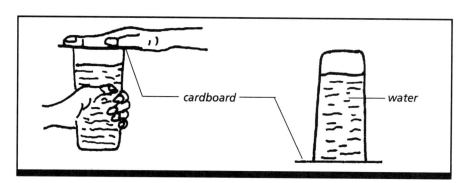

cardboard — water

Topic • Air pressure

Materials • A clear glass or plastic cup, a thin piece of cardboard or posterboard slightly larger than the mouth of the glass or a small plastic or Styrofoam plate, water, copy of the Upside-Down Glass of Water Application Sheet.

Demonstration

1. Introduce the materials to the students. Have a student volunteer fill the glass <u>completely</u> with water and place the cardboard on top of it. Ask the students to guess what will happen when the glass is turned upside down.

2. Have a new student volunteer place one hand on top of the cardboard while carefully turning the glass upside-down. A little water will drip out, so don't do this over a desk or a student's head.

3. Have the student slowly remove the hand that was holding the cardboard in place.

Analysis • Have the students tell or write what happened in the demonstration. Encourage them to explore these questions: *What keeps the water in the glass? What holds the cardboard in place? Can the glass be held sideways?*

Application • The students may read the story "The Jar of Poison" (from the Application Sheet) aloud or silently or listen to you read it. They may want to work in pairs or individually to finish the story. Have the students share their endings. Encourage them to make connections with what they learned about air pressure.

Explanation • When the glass was filled with water, there was no air left inside it. The glass contained no air, just water. Then, when the glass was slowly turned upside down, a little water dripped out but no air got inside the glass. This made a partial **vacuum**, which kept the cardboard attached to the mouth of the glass. The water stayed in the glass because the air pressure surrounding the glass was greater than the weight of the water. Air pressure pushed against the cardboard and kept the water in the glass. We could turn the glass upside down and sideways without having the water pour out because air pressure pushes in all directions.

THE UPSIDE-DOWN
• GLASS OF WATER •

Read the following story and write an ending for it. Remember what you learned in the Upside-Down Glass of Water demonstration.

The Jar of Poison

Once upon a time there was a poor family who lived in a tiny house next to a man who was very rich and very bad. The bad man was famous for the tricks he played on other people. One day he came to the poor family's house. He said, "I have bought the land your house is built on. You will have to move to a new place."

The father said. "No, please don't make us move. We are very poor and we will not be able to find a new house." The rich man said, " Well, there is one thing you can do to stay. I have a jar here of this special poison. If it touches your skin, you will disappear. If you really want to stay in this place, you will have to show that you are brave and smart."

"How do I do that?" asked the father. "You will turn this jar of liquid upside down above your son's head. If you can do this without harming your son, you can stay. If your son disappears, you will have to leave." The father thought about it. He loved his son very much and did not want to put him in danger. He thought some more. "I'll do it," he said. Then he…

II. HEAVY NEWS

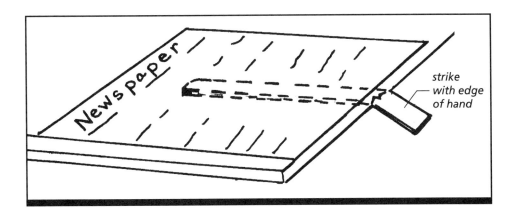

strike with edge of hand

Topic • Air pressure

Materials • A newspaper and a yardstick or similar piece of wood, at least two feet long. (Note: the wood will be broken in the demonstration.)

Demonstration

1. Lay the wood on a table with the end of the wood hanging 4–5 inches off the edge of the table. Ask the class to guess what will happen if someone hits the protruding end of the stick. Ask one of the students to hit the stick. What happened?

2. Place the stick back on the table and cover it with the newspaper. The edge of the newspaper should be even with the edge of the table. The stick should protrude as before. Ask the students to guess what will happen if you hit the stick.

3. Smooth the paper down with one hand and hit the stick with the edge of the other hand. Ask the students to report what happened.

4. The demonstration may be repeated by pulling the stick out 4–5 inches more.

Analysis • Divide the students into pairs. Tell them to talk about what they saw and to write a description. Put pairs together in fours to compare their descriptions. Have each group report to the whole class.

Application • Have the students work with partners or in a small group to think of as many examples as they can that show how strong air is. They can list them or draw them. If students have difficulty thinking of examples, suggest that they start with kinds of storms. Tires and balloons represent other examples. Have each group present their examples to the class.

Explanation • At the beginning of the demonstration, the stick was on the table. First a student hit the stick and it flew up in the air. Then the teacher put the newspaper on top of the stick, smoothed down the paper and hit the stick. This time the stick broke. What was different? The newspaper does not seem to be heavy enough to hold down the stick. What was on top of the newspaper? Did you see anything?

Imagine that there was a heavy box placed on top of the newspaper. Would you expect the newspaper to move then? You probably would not because you could see that there was something on the newspaper. In this case, even though you can not see it, there is something on top of the newspaper: a column of air. Because the teacher made the paper smooth before hitting the stick, there was almost no air under the paper. The weight of the air on top of the paper held it down with so much pressure that the stick broke. From this demonstration you can see that air has weight.

12. PLASTIC BAG POWER

Topic • Air pressure

Materials • Plastic sandwich bags (not the type that seals shut), straws, tape, books. You will need two bags and straws for the initial demonstration and one per student for the group work.

Demonstration

1. Show the students a plastic bag and a book. Tell them that you are going to move the book with the bag. Ask them to suggest ways you could do it.

2. Take out the straw and tape. Put the end of the straw in the bag so that it extends approximately two inches inside the bag. Use the tape to seal the bag closed around the straw.

3. Place a book on top of the bag and blow into the straw. As the bag inflates, the book will be pushed off and slide away.

4. Ask a volunteer to help you with the next part of the demonstration. Have her seal a straw in another bag in the same way you did the first one. Place both bags on a table with the straws extending from opposite ends. Place a book on top of the bags. Ask the students to predict what will happen this time. Blow into both straws at the same time. What happens to the book?

5. Divide the students into groups of three or four. (Preferably, all groups should have the same number of students.) Give each student a bag, a straw, and some tape. Each group should have a stack of books. Each group will work together using all their bags to see how many books they can lift. Have them keep track of their results. Are there other objects in the room they can lift with their bags?

The figure shows a plastic bag with a straw inserted and taped at the top, labeled "straw" and "plastic bag", with arrows indicating air flow into the bag.

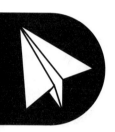

Analysis • Have each group share their results. Which group was able to lift the most books? Did anyone try to lift other objects? How can the air in the bag lift heavy objects?

Application • Have the students work in groups to brainstorm all the examples of compressed air they can. Ask them to share their lists with the rest of the class.

Explanation • As you blow air into the plastic bag through the straw, it is *compressed*, or squeezed into a smaller space. When air is compressed, it pushes harder on the inside of its container. The air pressure on the inside of the container is higher than the air pressure on the outside. This creates enough force to lift up the books in this demonstration. Air pressure in tires holds up cars and bicycles.

13. DRINKING RACE WITH STRAWS

Topic • Air pressure

Materials • For each pair of volunteers: two straws, one of which should be punctured with a few needle holes along its entire length, and two small cups and water or some other drinkable liquid.

Demonstration

1. Introduce the materials to the students and ask them to guess what kind of race they are going to have.

2. Select four pairs of volunteers from the class.

3. Give each pair two straws and two cups containing liquid. Be sure one pair member has a perforated straw and the other has one that is not perforated. Tell them that the first person to empty the cup will win the race. Do not tell the students that the straws are not the same.

4. Begin the race on the count of three.

5. Ask the students who are watching to tell what happened.

Analysis • Have the students tell what happened. Was it a fair race? Pass the straws around and have the students compare them. Which ones were the winning straws? Why was it so difficult to drink through the losing straws?

Application • A vacuum cleaner works on the same principle as a straw. A fan pumps the air out of the hose. Then the pressure of the atmosphere pushes air into the vacuum cleaner, along with dust and dirt. If there is a hole in the hose, the cleaner will not clean effectively.

Show the class the labeled drawing of a vacuum cleaner. Ask the students to try to explain how it works. What happens if there is a hole in the hose?

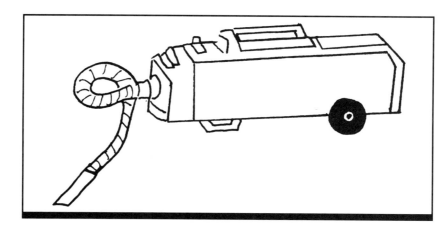

Explanation • When you sucked on the straw, you lowered the air pressure inside of it. This low pressure made a partial vacuum above the liquid. The air in the room, which had higher pressure, pushed down on the water in the glass. The water moved into the place with less air pressure: the straw. If you had the straw with the holes in it, you could not make a partial vacuum. You just sucked in air.

Force and Motion

14. BALLOON ROCKETS

Topic • Action/reaction

Materials • Two pieces of fishing line or thin string as long as the room, one copy of the Balloon Rockets Application Sheet for each person; for each group of three students: one balloon (all groups should have balloons of the same size and shape), one drinking straw, masking tape. There should be a few extra balloons and straws.

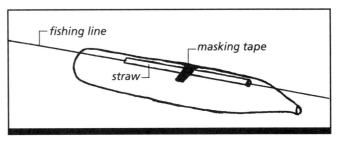

Demonstration

1. Explain to the students that they are going to have a race. Introduce the materials and ask them to guess the kind of race they are going to have.

2. Divide the class into groups of three and hand out the materials.

3. Have each student take a role: one will blow up and hold the end of the balloon, the second will hold the straw against the balloon, and the third will tape it on.

4. Explain and model the construction of the balloon rocket. Tell the students to blow up the balloon and then tape the straw to the balloon. It is important that the student holding the balloon keep the end of the balloon pinched tightly.

5. Begin the race. Two groups will compete at a time. Have two students from each group take the ends of the pieces of string and thread the string through the straws on two of the balloons. Those who are holding the strings then go to opposite ends of the room and hold the strings taut. The third student from the group continues to hold the end of their balloon. The balloons are put at the starting point at one end of each string. The holders release the balloons. The race continues until every group has had at least one chance to race its balloon.

Analysis • Have the students tell what happened. Why did one balloon go farther or faster than another? Which way did the air go? If you used longer string, would the balloons get to the end of it? When would the balloons stop moving?

Application • Pass out the application sheets. Have the students read or listen to the passages. Then tell them to draw a picture based on the reading and their own knowledge. Divide the students in groups and have them share their drawings. Ask each group to choose one to be presented and explained to the class. If possible, have pictures of rockets and jets available to encourage further conversation.

Explanation • When you blew up the balloon, you filled it with air. The air pressure inside the balloon was greater than the pressure outside the balloon. When you held the balloon shut, it did not move. Later, when you let go of the balloon, the air rushed out. The balloon flew across the room. Because it was attached to the straw and the string, it went in a straight line. The force of the air rushing out made the balloon move. This demonstrates **Newton's Third Law of Motion**, which says that for every action there is an equal and opposite **reaction**. When the air rushes out of the balloon, it pushes on the air around it. That is the action. This action of the air moving in one direction causes a reaction: the balloon moves in the opposite direction.

Follow-up • Bring in balloons of different sizes and shapes and let the groups choose the one they want to try. Some may want to try making double balloon rockets. The class could also experiment with different types (cotton string, fishing line) and lengths of string, perhaps going outdoors or into the corridor for longer races.

• BALLOON ROCKETS •

1. Everyone has seen pictures of rockets. Small rockets are used to send fireworks into the air. Large rockets are used for space travel and exploration. How do rockets work? A rocket has an open end and a closed end. Inside the rocket, at the closed end, there is fuel, which burns and creates hot gases. These gases push on the walls inside the rocket. They rush out of the rocket the only way they can, through the open end. When the hot gases come out, they push against the ground. This action of pushing causes an opposite reaction and the rocket leaves the ground.

Draw a picture of a rocket. Show how it works.

2. Jet planes also operate on the principle of action and reaction. Jet planes have big fans, which turn and pull air in through the front of the engine. The air is heated and it expands, or takes up more space. It goes out through the back with great force, pushing the airplane forward.

Draw a picture of a jet plane. Show how it works.

15. BALANCING ACTS

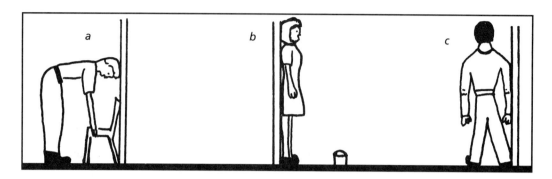

Topic • Center of gravity

Materials • For each group: one straight-backed chair, a can or cup, one set of Balancing Acts Direction Cards.

Demonstration

1. Divide the students into groups of three. For each activity one group member will read the directions, one will perform the task, and the third will write down observations.

2. Give each student a direction card and tell them not to show it to the other group members. The person who has Card 1 will begin by reading the directions to the person who has Card 2. The holder of Card 3 will write down observations. After completing the first task, the roles will switch and the group will work with Card 2 and then Card 3.

Analysis • After the students have finished and written down their observations, have them look for similarities among the tasks. Then discuss them with the whole class. You may want to provide the words **balance** and **center of gravity** and demonstrate them.

Application • Ask the students if they have ever watched workers constructing a tall building. In order to lift their materials, builders use a tall machine called a *crane*. Divide the students in pairs and have them draw a picture of a crane. As the students draw, encourage them to compare their drawings with each others' and with real cranes or pictures of them. As they do so, be sure they notice the weights on the crane which balance the heavy loads. Where are the weights located? Why doesn't the crane fall over when it picks up heavy building materials? How does that relate to the demonstrations?

Explanation • You did three experiments. In the first one, the person stood with her feet against the wall. Then she tried to bend over and pick up an object from the floor. It was impossible to do it without falling down unless she bent her knees or moved away from the wall. The second person stood with his right foot and right shoulder against the wall. Then he tried to move his left foot. He could not do it. When he turned and put his left foot and shoulder against the wall and tried to lift his right foot, it was still impossible. In the third experiment, the person took two steps away from a wall and then leaned over to pick up a chair. Some people were able to do this and some were not. Did you notice that women or girls could do it but men or boys could not?

All three of the experiments you did are related to the **center of gravity** in your body. **Gravity** is the force which holds us to the earth. It gives us weight. The center of gravity is the point at which all of an object's weight seems to be concentrated. You know that if you hold an object such as a ruler in the middle, it will balance. The center of gravity may not be in the middle of all objects, but there will always be a point, called the **center of gravity**, where an object will balance. You can change the center of gravity by adding weight to one part of the object.

• BALANCING ACTS •

DIRECTION CARDS

Card 1

Go to a wall and stand with your toes touching it. Take two steps away (measure them toe to heel with your shoes on). Bend over straight from the hips and put your head against the wall. Ask someone to hand you a chair with its back against the wall. Lift the chair with your head still against the wall. Try to straighten up while still holding the chair. If you are a male, ask a female to try it next. If you are a female, ask a male to try it.

Card 2

Go to a wall and stand straight with your back against it. Have someone put the cup or can about 8 to 12 inches in front of you on the floor. Pick up the object from the floor without bending your knees.

Card 3

Go to a wall and stand straight next to it. Put your right foot and right shoulder against the wall. Now try to lift or move your left leg. Turn the other way and put your left foot and left shoulder against the wall. Try to lift or move your right foot.

16. HANG THE HAMMER

Topic • Center of gravity

Materials • A hammer with a wooden handle, a ruler, a short piece of string; for the Application: each group will need two cardboard tubes (toilet paper

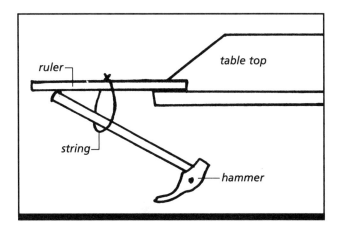

tubes are fine), two index cards, scissors and glue, and a copy of the Hang the Hammer Application Sheet.

Demonstration

1. Show the students the hammer, the ruler, and the string. Have them tell you about each item as you show it. Do not show them the picture at this point. Do the demonstration in a place where there is space under the table to accommodate the hammer hanging down and where the students can clearly see the demonstration.

2. Place the ruler so that it is hanging over the edge of a desk or table. Invite the students to test how secure the ruler is by pushing down on it. Does it support the weight? Why not?

3. Have volunteer students test the weight of the hammer. Ask them if they can hang the hammer on the ruler using the string. Let them take turns trying.

4. If no one has succeeded, demonstrate how it can be done, using an unlabeled copy of the picture above to help you. Let the students take turns hanging the hammer on the ruler. Ask them to guess why it works.

Analysis • Have the students draw a side view of the hanging hammer showing exactly where the following are: the hammer handle, the hammer head, the ruler, the edge of the table, the string. Ask them to label each part of the drawing. As the students are drawing, walk around to be sure that they are drawing an exact picture of the hanging hammer.

Application • Divide the students into groups of three. Hand out the application sheet. Tell the students they are going to make a bridge. You may want to talk about the picture of it before you start.

Explanation • Put the hammer down on the table with the wooden handle touching the edge. Now move the wooden handle of the hammer gradually over the edge of the table. The hammer will not fall off the table until the iron head of the hammer reaches the edge. If you reverse this procedure , and put the head of the hammer closest to the edge of the table, the hammer will fall as soon as the iron head crosses the edge. This is because the **center of gravity** of the hammer is in the iron part. The head is heavier than the handle. This puts the point at which the weight of the hammer is balanced closer to the head end than to the middle or to the handle end.

Now look at the diagram you drew showing the position of the hammer, ruler, table edge and the string. The head of the hammer (that is, the center of gravity) is directly under where the ruler is on the table. This is called the *pivot point*. A system can only be stable if the center of gravity is under the pivot point.

• HANG THE HAMMER •

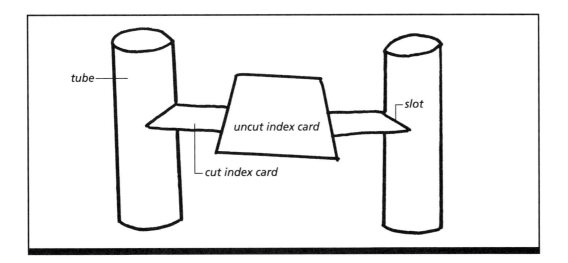

tube

slot

uncut index card

cut index card

You are going to make a model of a special kind of bridge called a *cantilever bridge*. How is the bridge special? How does it stay up? Where is its center of gravity? Look at the picture and follow the directions. You will need the following materials: two cardboard tubes, two index cards, scissors, and glue.

1. Cut a slot in each tube $\frac{1}{3}$ of the way down from the top of the tube.

2. Cut one of the index cards in half lengthwise. This makes two thin rectangles.

3. Push one end of one of the rectangles into the slot in one of the tubes.

4. Do the same with the other rectangle and the other tube. These will make the supports for the bridge.

5. Finally, glue the uncut index card onto the two supporting cards to finish the bridge.

6. Think of ways you could make the bridge stronger and more stable.

17. WRONG WAY?

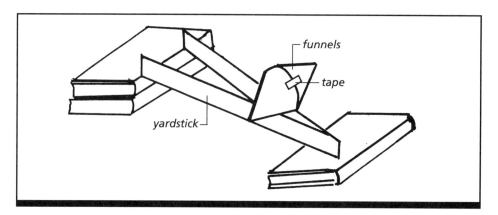

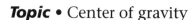

Topic • Center of gravity

Materials • Two yard or meter sticks, three books (each at least one inch thick), masking tape, two funnels of equal size. For the Application: each group will need a tissue box and a small, heavy weight. (A fishing weight works well.)

Demonstration

1. Put two books 30 inches (90 cm.) apart on the floor. Have a student use one of the yardsticks to measure the distance.

2. Put the third book on top of one of the other books.

3. Place the yardsticks on top of the books to make a letter V, with the open part of the V on the two books.

4. Tape the bowls of the funnels together.

5. Put the funnels at the bottom of the V. Ask the students to guess what will happen. Let the funnels go.

Analysis • Ask the students to tell what happened. Were they surprised that the funnels went "up the hill?" Why? Do they have an explanation for what they saw? Repeat the demonstration and have the students look at the funnels in relation to the floor. Are the funnels closer to the floor or farther from it at the end?

Application • Divide the students into groups of three or four. Tell them that they are going to design a magic box which will balance on the edge of a table. (You may want to make one in advance to demonstrate.) Give each group a tissue box and a small, heavy weight. Have them work together in their groups to make a box which will balance. Then have each group invent a story they could tell as they show others their magic boxes. The groups can present their stories to the class and choose the best one, or they could go to other classes to present their magic boxes and stories.

Explanation • When you put the funnels on the V shape formed by the measuring sticks, they seemed to go uphill, against the pull of gravity. But was that really what happened? As they reached the wider part of the V, the heavier part of the funnels moved closer to the floor.

18. SLIDES

Topic • Friction

Materials • A piece of wood (such as a large cutting board) which can be used as a slide for objects; a metal tray or cookie sheet for the same purpose; five objects for sliding: a flat pencil eraser, an ice cube, a stone, a small piece of wood (such as a child's building block), and a small matchbox or jewelry box; copy of the Slides Analysis and Application Sheet.

Demonstration

1. Ask the students to tell you what they think of when they hear the word *slide.* You might encourage them by drawing a picture of a playground slide. Ask them to share experiences with slides. Write the words *fast* and *slow* on the board. What are some things that make a difference between a slow ride on a slide and a fast one?

2. Hand out the analysis/application sheet. Have students fill in the names of the objects on the chart as you show them to the class.

3. Show them the board and the metal tray and explain that they will be used as slides.

4. In the Wood-Prediction column, have the students number their predictions about which object will reach the bottom of the slide first. On what did they base their predictions? Was there general agreement? Have volunteers place the objects at the top of the board. Have one student slowly tip the board up so that the objects begin to move. Record the results in the appropriate boxes. Repeat with the metal tray.

Analysis • Record the results from the analysis chart on the board or on a large poster. Encourage the students to discuss their predictions and the results.

Application • Have the students work in pairs to complete the Application portion of the sheet. After about 5 minutes, ask them to share their observations about friction with their classmates.

Explanation • When you used the board as a slide, the objects moved more slowly than they did on the metal sheet. On both surfaces, the smoother objects moved faster than the rougher ones.

When two rough or uneven surfaces rub against each other, an invisible force called **friction** slows them down and makes it harder for them to move. The less friction there is between surfaces, the more easily the objects move.

Name_____

• SLIDES •

Analysis

Object	Wood Prediction	Wood Result	Metal Prediction	Metal Result
1.				
2.				
3.				
4.				
5.				

Applicaton

Friction: Helpful or Not? Sometimes friction is helpful and sometimes it is not. Look at the following examples of friction with your partner. Try to decide how friction works in the example. Is it helpful or isn't it? Write *H* in front of the examples where it is helpful and *N* in front of the ones where it is not.

Examples of Friction

____ Kicking a ball

____ Writing with a pencil

____ Driving a car into the wind

____ Putting tape on a baseball bat

____ Using hand brakes on a bike

____ Turning a doorknob

____ Wearing rubber soled shoes for dancing

____ Climbing rocks

____ Wearing leather-soled shoes on ice

Can you think of other examples of friction?

19. ROLLERS

Topic • Friction

> **Note.** This lesson is a follow-up to Lesson 18, Slides, as both deal with friction. The Analysis assumes students will have done both.

Materials • A large, unopened can (be sure it has a ridge running around the outer edge), six to eight marbles, a book.

Demonstration

1. Show the students the can and the book. Ask if anyone can spin the book around on top of the can. Have some volunteers try it.

2. Show the students the marbles. Ask them how the marbles could be used to make the book spin. Have the students try out their suggestions. If no one else suggests it, place the marbles around the outer rim of the can and put the book on top of it. Then spin the book.

Analysis • Review Lesson 18, Slides. Have the students tell you what they have learned about friction. Then ask them to relate the roller demonstration to their previous knowledge.

Application • Divide the students into groups and ask them to consider the following:

In ancient Egypt and in South America at the time of the Inca Empire, when people had to move very large stones long distances, they put tree trunks under the loads of stones. Why do you think they did that? How does it relate to the demonstration?

Explanation • When you tried to spin the book on top of the can, you could not do it. This was because there was too much **friction**, or rubbing, between the book and the can. When you put the marbles between the book and the can, there was less friction. The places where the marbles actually touch the book and the can are very small, so the friction is very low. Many machines use ball bearings to reduce friction. They work just the way the marbles did in this demonstration.

20. PUT THE COIN IN THE CUP

Topic • Inertia

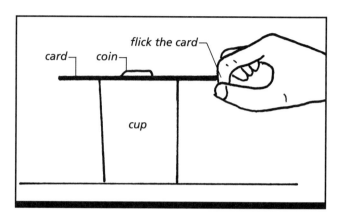

Materials • For each group of students: an index card, a coin, and a cup or glass. (Don't use plastic, foam, or paper cups, as they are too light.)

Demonstration

1. Give each group of students a card, a coin, and a cup. Have them place the card on the cup, and place the coin on the card.

2. Tell them that their job is to figure out a way to get the coin to drop into the cup without touching the coin or picking up the card.

Analysis • Have the groups keep a record on paper of the attempts they make to solve the problem, listing each one (*Trial 1, Trial 2,* etc.), what they did, and how it turned out. Then ask the students to report back on their results.

Application • Divide the students in small groups and present the following, either orally or in writing

When you are riding in a car or bus and it moves forward with a sudden motion, you are pushed backwards. Why does this happen? What happens when the car stops suddenly? How does this relate to the demonstration? Can you think of other examples of inertia?

If the students seem to have difficulty thinking of other examples of inertia, you might suggest such common ones as rolling balls. After the groups have had time to consider these questions, ask them to share their thoughts with the whole class.

Explanation • At first it seems that there is no way to get the coin into the cup without touching the coin or picking up the card. It is clear that the problem is to get the card out of the way. As you discovered, however, if you flicked the card hard with your finger, the card moved but the coin did not. This event shows a common characteristic that all objects have, which is called **inertia. Inertia** means that objects which are at rest tend to stay at rest. We could see that, when we moved the card quickly, the coin stayed in one place. The more quickly the card is moved, the more likely it is that the coin will not move with it. *Inertia* also means that when an object is moving, it will tend to continue moving. This is one of **Newton's Laws of Motion.**

21. FINGER POWER

Topic • Levers

Materials • For each Group A pair: four books, two sharpened pencils, copy of the Group A Direction Card; for each Group B pair: several toothpicks, copy of the Group B Direction Card.

Demonstration

1. Divide the students into two groups, Group A and Group B. Give each group their materials. Have the students work in pairs within their groups. As the students are working, walk around and have them tell you what they have observed. They may want to draw it.

2. Put all the Group A students and all the Group B students together and ask them to decide how to present their demonstrations and observations to the whole class.

Analysis • Have the students present their demonstrations and observations to the class.

Application • Ask the students to consider the following ordinary household items and see if they can connect them to the demonstrations:

- a hammer or crowbar when it is used to pull out nails
- a nutcracker
- a wheelbarrow
- scissors
- pliers

Ask them to think of any other tools that use levers.

Explanation • In these demonstrations, you were using simple machines called **levers**. A lever makes the force you use stronger, more powerful. It makes it easier to move or lift things.

The lever Group A used to lift the books was made with two pencils. The pencil lying next to the books acts as the *fulcrum*, or rotation point. The pencil they pushed on is called the *arm*. When they pushed at the end of the arm, they were applying force farther from the fulcrum. This made it easier to move the books. If they used a shorter pencil, they had to apply more force because they were pushing closer to the fulcrum. When they moved the fulcrum (the second pencil) farther from the book, they had to push harder. But, did you notice that the books went up higher?

Group B also used a lever, their fingers. The fulcrum was the place where their fingers joined their hands. When the toothpick was far from the fulcrum, at the fingertips, it was very difficult to break it. When it was closer to the fulcrum, the work was easier.

• FINGER POWER •

DIRECTION CARDS

Group A

1. Stack the books.

2. Try to lift the books with your little finger. Have your partners try it. Is it easy to do?

3. How could you use the pencils to help you lift the books?

4. Push the pointed end of one of the pencils under the bottom book. Put the second pencil under the first near the edge of the book.

5. Push down on the first pencil with your little finger. Is it still hard to lift the books?

6. Try using different lengths of pencil.

7. Try moving the second pencil farther from the book.

Group B

1. Put a toothpick across the back of your middle finger near the ends of your fingers, under the first and third finger. Try to break the toothpick by pressing down with your first and third fingers. Can you break it?

2. Little by little, move the toothpick closer to your hand and try to break it at various points. When does it break most easily?

22. IT'S A SNAP

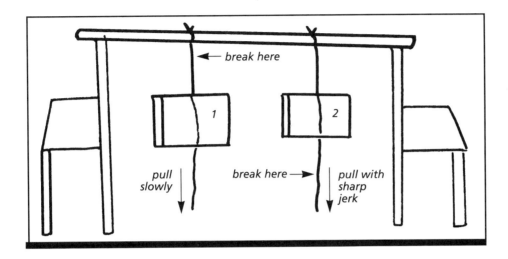

Topic • Strain

Materials • Two paperback books about the same thickness, sewing thread, a broomstick or a sturdy yardstick. (The yardstick should not bend.)

Demonstration

1. Place the yardstick between two bookcases or the backs of two chairs. Have two students hold down the ends of the yardstick to prevent it from moving. Be sure the yardstick is level.

2. Cut two eighteen-inch lengths of thread. Tie one end of each thread to the yardstick.

3. Loop the thread around each book. Tie a knot below the books. The books should hang side-by-side with about six inches of thread above and below them.

4. To make it easier for your students to identify each book, give each of the books a name (Book 1 and Book 2). Ask your students to answer the following questions. Encourage guessing.

If I pull slowly on the thread of Book 1, where will the thread break? Above or below the book? (Answer: above)

If I pull with a quick jerk on the thread of Book 2, where will the thread break? Above or below the book? (Answer: below)

5. Now perform the demonstration as described in the questions.

Analysis • Ask your students to explain what happened. These questions can be asked of small groups or of the whole class: Why does pulling slowly on the thread cause it to break above the book? Why does a quick jerk cause the thread to break below the book? Does the weight of the book help to break the thread? Why? Why not?

Application • After the students have seen or heard the explanation, have the class look at a copy of the following picture of the car being towed.

Introduce the following information either orally or in writing.

When people need to tow (pull) a parked car, they must pull slowly. Pulling slowly allows the cable between the cars to receive the strain evenly along the cable's entire length. If the parked car is pulled too quickly, the strain on the cable will be too great and, like the thread, the cable will break.

What did you learn in the demonstration which will help explain this?

Explanation • When you pulled the thread slowly, a strain was placed along its entire length, both above and below the book. Since the weight of the book added to the pull, the strain was greater above the book and the thread broke above the book. When you pulled with a quick jerk, there was not enough time for the strain to travel up past the book. Most of the strain remained concentrated below the book and the thread broke below it.

ELECTRICITY AND MAGNETISM

23. MAKING ELECTRICITY

Topic • Static electricity

Materials • For Station 1: balloons, string or rubber bands to tie the ends (if desired), copy of the Station 1 Direction Card; for Station 2: balloons, string or rubber bands to tie the ends (if desired), thread, thin sticks, copy of the Station 2 Direction Card.; for Station 3: plastic combs (students may supply their own), tiny scraps of tissue paper or other thin paper, copy of the Station 3 Direction Card.

Demonstration • In this demonstration, the students will be located at three different stations. At each station there should be a direction card as well as the materials in amounts sufficient for one third of the class to work at the station at a time.

1. Tell the students that they are going to do some demonstrations about electricity. Ask them to tell you what words they think of when they hear the word *electricity*. List the words on the board.

2. Assign students in pairs to stations. Ask them to do the demonstraton as directed on the direction card. Give them unlined paper on which to draw their observations.

Analysis • Have the students, working in pairs, draw a picture of each demonstration. Ask the groups to describe their drawings to the class. Encourage them to speculate about the reasons for what they observed.

Application • Divide the students in pairs or small groups to make a list of experiences they have had with static electricity. Encourage them to use details to tell about their experiences: Where were they? Exactly what happened? Some common examples might be touching another person and getting a shock or having clothes stick to the wearer or to each other. Have each group choose one incident to tell the class.

Explanation • The three demonstrations you did are all examples of **static electricity**. Static electricity is different from the kind of

electricity you are familiar with, which flows through wires. Static electricity stays in one place. Thunder and lightning are caused by static electricity. So are the sparks you see, feel, or hear when you walk across a carpet and then touch something metal.

In the first demonstration, the balloon stuck to the wall. By rubbing the balloon, you created an electrical charge on the balloon. There was a difference between the charge on the balloon (negative) and the charge on the wall (positive). If electrical charges are the same, they push away from each other; but if they are opposites, they attract each other. For that reason, the balloon was pulled against the wall. If you left it there long enough, it would fall down.

In the second demonstration, you rubbed both balloons. They both had the same kind of static charge. Things that have the same kind of charge try to *repel* or push away from each other.

The third demonstration is like the first. It shows how an object with a negative static charge, the comb, attracts objects with a positive static charge, the pieces of paper.

• MAKING ELECTRICITY •

Station 1: Sticky Balloons

Blow up a balloon and tie the end closed. Rub the balloon
several times on your hair or clothes. Hold it against the
wall. Then let go of the balloon. What happens?

Station 2: Unfriendly Balloons

Blow up two balloons and tie the ends closed. Then tie the
two balloons together with a piece of thread about 8 inches
long. Have one person hold the piece of wood while the
other hangs the thread over the wood so that the two balloons are next to each other. Rub one of the balloons hard
against your hair or clothes. Let go of the balloons. What
happens to them? Now rub both balloons. Is the result the
same?

Station 3: Sticky Paper

Rub the comb several times on your clothes or your hair.
Then hold the comb close to the pieces of paper. What
happens to the paper?

DIRECTION CARDS

24. LOOK! NO HANDS!

Topic • Static electricity

> **Note:** This should be used as a follow-up to Lesson 23, Making Electricity.

Materials • A small piece of modeling clay (available in toy departments or hobby shops), a pushpin, a one-inch square of tissue paper, a clear plastic glass, an inflated balloon small enough to hold in your hand; for each student: a copy of the Look! No Hands! Application Sheet.

Demonstration

1. Show the students the modeling clay and the pushpin. Ask a volunteer to push the end of the pin in the clay with the point upward. Ask another volunteer to fold the tissue paper square in half like a tent and balance it on the pin point. Place the plastic glass over the pin and the paper tent. Keep the balloon hidden.

2. Ask the students to suggest ways to take the paper tent off the pin without moving the glass. Take out the balloon. Ask if it could be used to move the tent.

3. Have a volunteer rub the balloon on her hair. Continue to elicit suggestions from the students. Ask the volunteer to hold the balloon near to but not touching the plastic glass. At the same time, tell the students to watch the tent. The tent will turn and fall off the pushpin.

Analysis • Ask the students to recall the demonstrations they did earlier in Lesson 23, Making Electricity. You may want to sketch each part of it to help them recall what happened. Then ask them how they think the previous demonstrations relate to this one. How was the balloon able to move the tissue paper?

Application • Ask the students to tell you what they know about thunderstorms. Then have the students work individually or in pairs with the application sheet to match each stage of a thunderstorm to the appropriate picture.

Explanation • Why did the paper tent fall off the pushpin? When you rubbed one side of the balloon, that side picked up electrons from your hair. The balloon became negatively charged. The negatively charged balloon attracted the positive part of the paper tent. The attraction was strong enough to pull the tent off the pushpin.

Name_____

• LOOK! NO HANDS! •

Each of these paragraphs is about a different stage in the development of a thunderstorm. Match each picture with the correct description.

_____ **1.** Thunderstorms usually happen during the summer, when the air is warm and wet. As the warm, damp air rises, it becomes cooler. The water it holds forms large, dark thunderclouds.

_____ **2.** Inside each thundercloud, there are air currents. These air currents move quickly and cause positive and negative electric charges to build up.

_____ **3.** The electricity is released from the clouds as giant sparks. We call these giant sparks *lightning*.

_____ **4.** When lightning leaves a cloud, it zig-zags to the ground. Then it goes back up the same path to the cloud. What we see is the lightning returning to the cloud, the *return stroke*.

25. MAGNETIC ATTRACTION

Topic • Magnetism

Materials • For Station 1: a strong magnet and an assortment of things to test: paper clips, keys, an eraser, a pencil, aluminum foil, coins, plastic or glass containers, small rocks, and nails, copy of the Station 1 Direction Card; for Station 2: a strong magnet, plastic bag, cardboard, aluminum foil, paper, handkerchief, tacks or paper clips, copy of the Station 2 Direction Card; for Station 3: three or four magnets of different strengths (refrigerator magnets are fine), a ruler, paper clips, copy of the Station 3 Direction Card.

Demonstration

1. In this demonstration, students will explore aspects of magnetic force. Ask them to tell you what words they think of when they hear the word *magnet*. List the words on the board.

2. Students should be located at three different stations. There should be a direction card and a sufficient amount of materials at each station. The students should also have paper on which to chart the results of their investigations.

Analysis • Have the students work in small groups to compare their observations about magnetic attraction. Then ask each group to present the results of their investigations to the class. Encourage students to discuss the possible reasons for what they observed.

Application • In the same small groups, have the students make a list of uses for magnets. Ask them to draw upon their own experiences as well as on their knowledge of science and technology. Have the groups compare their lists. Do they agree on all of them? If there are areas of disagreement, the students can be encouraged to use the school library to find out who is right.

Explanation • All three demonstrations explore aspects of *magnetic force*, the force that attracts certain metals.

In the first demonstration, you observed that only the objects made of the metals iron, steel, and nickel stick to the magnet.

The other items, even other metals such as copper or aluminum, do not stick at all.

In the second demonstration, magnetic force is almost completely unaffected by the materials a magnet does not attract. This is why magnets can be used to attach paper notes to a refrigerator door. Their force passes right through the paper and paint. However, many layers of paper or cloth can stop a magnet from working, because the thickness of the materials keeps the metal objects beyond the reach of the magnet's force field.

In the third demonstration, a stronger magnet can attract an object at a greater distance than a weaker one. This occurs because a stronger magnet has a stronger **magnetic field**. In the case of the vertical ruler, the magnet cannot pull the paper clip as far as before because the force of **gravity** is pulling the paper clip down.

• MAGNETIC ATTRACTION •

Station 1

Touch the magnet to each of the objects on the table. Make a chart by writing down the name of each object and the result: *sticks/does not stick*. Separate the objects that stick to the magnet from the other items.

What is similar about the objects that stick?

Station 2

To see what materials magnetic force will pass through, wrap the magnet in each of the materials on the table.

Will the wrapped magnet attract the tacks or paper clips? Now, see if the magnet will work through folded layers of paper, cloth, or plastic. Write down your observations.

Station 3

Investigate how far different magnets can pull a paper clip. Place a ruler flat on a table. Then, place a paper clip at zero (0) and the magnet six inches away. Slowly push the magnet toward the paper clip, waiting a few seconds at each ruler mark. When the paper clip sticks to the magnet, write down how far it traveled. Try this test with different magnets, writing down the results.

Next, hold the ruler up vertically against the edge of a table, so zero is level with the table top. Again place the paper clip at zero. Use the strongest magnet you have, and slowly slide it down the ruler until the paper clip jumps up. Now, compare the distance the paper clip traveled vertically with the earlier (flat on the table) results. Are the measurements the same? Why or why not?

DIRECTION CARDS

26. MAKE A COMPASS

Topic • Magnetism

> **Note.** Try this in the classroom before using it with the class to be sure the compass needle is not deflected by steel construction or equipment.

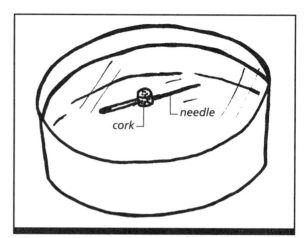

Materials • A large sewing needle, a small piece of cork or Styrofoam, a shallow bowl of water, a magnet, a colored marker.

Demonstration

1. Ask your students to decide which part of the classroom faces east. Remind them that the sun always rises in the east and sets in the west. After they have discussed this fact and come to an agreement, have a student stand facing east. North will be on her left, south on her right, and west behind her. Have the students write each cardinal direction on a piece of paper and attach it to the appropriate wall of the classroom.

2. Have the students sit in a circle so they can see the demonstration. To make a compass, ask a student volunteer to magnetize the needle by stroking one end of the magnet along the entire length of the needle in the same direction. Do this 20 times. Now place the magnetized needle on the small piece of cork or Styrofoam and carefully float it in a shallow bowl of water. (You may want to tape the needle to the cork/Styrofoam or make a groove in it with the needle to prevent it from rolling off.) The needle will swing around, pointing in a north-south direction. Mark the north end of the needle with the colored marker.

Analysis • Show the students an example of a compass rose. Using the homemade compass and the cardinal directions on your

classroom walls as their guide, ask your students to draw a compass rose on paper.

Application • Have your students look at maps. Familiarize them with the conventions of map making by pointing out that north is usually at the top. As an example, draw a picture on the board of your classroom in relation to another room or building at your school. Ask students to work in pairs to draw a map of their school or neighborhood. Remind them to show the cardinal directions (compass rose) on their maps. Then have the students present their maps to the class, pointing out the direction of buildings or rooms in relation to their classroom or home. For example: *The cafeteria is north of our classroom, but the library is south of it.*

Explanation • In this demonstration, you saw that a compass needle is actually a small magnet that lines up with the Earth's north-south magnetic field. This is because our planet acts as if it has a giant magnet running through the center of it with lines of magnetic force traveling around it from the north to the south pole. The Chinese were the first people to use magnets to help them find their way.

To turn the needle into a magnet, you first had to magnetize it. By stroking the needle with the magnet, you lined up the tiny particles that make up the metal all in the same direction. As long as the particles stay lined up and pointed in the same direction, the needle will act like a magnet. If you accidentally drop your needle, the particles may be shaken out of line and it will lose its magnetic force.

27. MAKE AN ELECTROMAGNET

Topic • Magnets

Materials • Two size D batteries, insulated (plastic-covered) copper wire 2 or 3 feet long and stripped ½ inch on each end to expose the copper wire, an iron or steel nail about 6 inches long, tape, a box of paper clips, a compass.

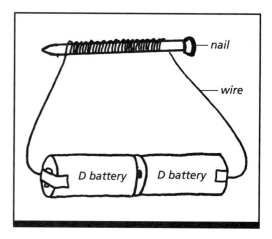

Demonstration

1. Have the students review what they know about magnets. How do you know if an object is a magnet? Can you make a magnet? (If they have done Lesson 24, Make a Compass, have a student tell how a magnet was made in that demonstration.) Show the students the materials and tell them you are going to make a magnet. Ask them to guess how it will be done.

2. Tape the two batteries together, joining the positive (+) and negative (–) ends. Tape one end of the wire to the positive end of the battery. (Be sure it is firmly attached to the metal button in the center of the positive end.) Wind the wire around the nail 10 or 15 times. Firmly tape the free end of the wire to the flat metal (negative) end of the battery.

3. Have your students test the nail with the paper clips to see if it is now magnetized. Another way to demonstrate the presence of a magnetic field is to have your students place a compass near the coiled wire and observe what happens to the compass needle.

Analysis • What happened to the nail? Have your students predict what will happen if you disconnect one end of the wire from the battery. Have a student volunteer disconnect the wire and place the end of the nail into the box of paper clips. What happens? Now, have a volunteer wind even more of the wire around the nail in tight coils. (You may need to tape some of the wire to hold it securely in place.) Reconnect the free end of the wire to the battery and test the magnet again. Does the extra wire make the magnet stronger or weaker? How do you know?

Application • Many electric appliances work by using electromagnetism. For example, the electric motors that run a fan, hair dryer, or electric clock have coils of wire inside of them that are positioned between the poles of a magnet. When an electric current flows through the coils, a magnetic field is produced which causes the coils to spin. These spinning coils are attached to rods with gears which run the appliances. Your students may want to go to the library and find diagrams of appliances which show how they work.

Explanation • Scientists have discovered many links between electricity and magnetism. When an electric current flows through a wire, it produces a **magnetic field**. In this demonstration, this field lined up the metal particles in the nail, turning it into a magnet. The more wire coils you added to the nail, the stronger the magnetic force became.

If your nail was made of iron, you discovered that the paper clips fell off the nail when the wire was disconnected. Iron remains magnetic only as long as an electric current runs through it. Iron forms a temporary magnet. But if your nail was made of steel, it remained magnetic even after the electric current was stopped. Steel forms a permanent magnet.

The magnetic field created by the electric current was also responsible for setting the compass needle spinning away from the north-south position.

28. PUSH/PULL

Topic • Magnetism

Materials • For Station 1: two strong bar magnets, iron filings (file down a large nail, get some at a machine shop, or buy them at a scientific supplies store), half a file folder (or paper of similar thickness), drawing paper, copy of the Station 1 Direction Card; for Station 2: two strong bar magnets, a small toy car, tape, copy of the Station 2 Direction Card; for Station 3: two strong bar magnets, two pencils, tape, copy of the Station 3 Direction Card; copy of the Push/Pull Application Reading.

Demonstration

1. Have the students review what they have learned about magnets. Tell them that they are going to explore the invisible forces that surround magnets.

2. Provide direction cards and materials at each station.

3. Divide the students into groups and assign each group to one station. Remind the students to record their observations. Each group will work at only one station.

Analysis • After the groups have finished their demonstrations, ask them to talk about their observations among themselves. Ask each group to perform its demonstration and to report its findings.

Application • Copy the application reading on an overhead transparency. Reveal the text one line at a time. As the class reads it together, ask the students to comment on what they read and to predict what else they will learn.

Explanation • The ends of magnets are called *poles* and every magnet has two types: a north pole and a south pole. Magnetic force is strongest at these poles. Different poles (north-south) pull together, or *attract* each other. The same poles (north-north, south-south) push apart, or *repel* each other.

Note: You may want to check for understanding by putting the following words on the board. Have one or more students draw and label a picture of magnets that illustrates what they have learned in these demonstrations.

north   push apart (repel)
south   pull together (attract)

• PUSH/PULL •

Station 1

1. Place half a file folder on a bar magnet. Sprinkle the iron filings evenly above the magnet. Carefully observe what happens. Draw a picture of the pattern the iron filings make.

2. Place the two bar magnets flat on the table with the two ends (poles) facing each other. Slowly push the ends together. Watch how the magnets move. Do they pull together? Do they push apart? Turn one of the magnets around and repeat the activity. Put the file folder on top of the magnets and sprinkle the iron filings above them. Draw a picture of the patterns the iron filings make—**a.** when they pull together, and **b.** when they push apart.

Station 2

Tape one magnet to the roof of the toy car. Take the other magnet and place its end (pole) near the end of the magnet taped to the car. What happens? Does the car roll forward or backward? Turn around the magnet you are holding. What happens now?

Station 3

Put the two pencils crosswise on top of a magnet. Put the other magnet on top of the pencils. If the top magnet pulls toward the bottom magnet, turn the ends around until you feel the two magnets push away from each other. Join the magnets with tape. Be sure to keep the tape loose. Now remove the pencils. Your top magnet will float above the bottom magnet!

• PUSH/PULL •

• The force that pushes away two of the same magnetic poles (north-north, south-south) is used in high speed trains.

• Two powerful magnets are created when a strong current of electricity flows through both the track and the train.

• The north pole of the train faces downward while the north pole of the track faces upward.

• When the electric current is turned on, the two north poles repel each other.

• This lifts the train so that it floats above the track.

• Because the train does not touch the track, there is no friction.

• Magnetic trains can travel at much higher speeds than ordinary trains with wheels.

APPLICATION READING

29. NOW YOU HEAR IT, NOW YOU DON'T

Topic • Radio waves

Materials • A battery-operated portable radio, aluminum foil.

Demonstration

1. Turn on the radio and tune it to a station with a clear signal.

2. Ask a student volunteer to help you. Have him tear off a piece of aluminum foil that is large enough to completely cover the radio and antenna.

3. Have another volunteer place the radio on top of the foil, then slowly lift the sides of the foil until they overlap above the radio. The aluminum foil will block the reception of radio waves and the radio will stop playing.

Analysis • Ask your students to discuss what happened. Why did the radio stop playing? How do radios work? What would happen if the antenna was left uncovered? What are radio waves?

Application • Together, electricity and magnetism make many things work for us. Electromagnetic radio waves bring music to your radio. Radio antennas receive radio waves which are turned into sound you can hear through the speaker. Because radio waves travel at the speed of light (186,300 miles a second), people who live a great distance apart can hear the same radio program at the same time.

Have your students tune the portable radio to a station with a weak signal. Have a student volunteer carry the radio to different locations around the classroom in search of better reception. Which parts of the room improve the reception of the radio waves? Near a window? In a corner? Beside the door?

Ask your students how this experience is related to the demonstration they performed with the aluminum foil.

Explanation • There are many kinds of electromagnetic waves. Radio waves are just one type. Radio waves are all around us. Radio **antennas** receive radio waves and change them into electrical signals which are then turned into sound by the speakers. By surrounding the radio with aluminum foil, we *neutralize* or block the radio waves. The radio suddenly stops receiving the electromagnetic signals it turns into sound.

Visual PERCEPTION

30. AFTER THE BELL

Topic • After images, complementary colors

Materials • A drawing of a bell with the outside colored yellow, the inside colored green and a black dot in the middle as shown in the picture. This should be on an 8½-by-11-inch sheet of paper. You will also need blank sheets of paper of the same size, markers, and paper for students.

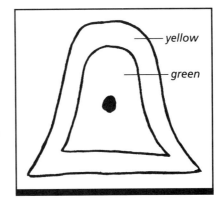

Demonstration

1. Put the bell picture up on the wall with the blank sheet of paper next to it.

2. Ask the students to stare at the black dot in the center of the bell for 20 seconds.

3. Tell them to look immediately at the middle of the blank sheet of paper. What do they see? Tell them that this is called an *after-image*.

4. Pass out paper and markers to the students. Assign each student a geometric shape to draw using two of the following colors: red, green, violet, yellow, blue, orange.

5. Post the drawings around the room, with a white piece of paper next to each one.

6. Have the students walk around the room and look at each picture for 20 seconds, then at the blank sheet next to it. Have them make notes on their analysis sheets. They may need to pause for a minute after each picture, since after-images tend to persist.

Analysis • Have the students fill out the analysis sheet and then share their observations. A chart can be made on the board.

Application • After the students have gone over the explanation and completely understand it, instruct them to use what they have learned to draw and color a picture of the United States flag in such a way that the after-image has the correct colors. You may want to have a flag or a picture of it in the room.

Explanation • White light is made up of all the colors you can see in a rainbow. It is possible to make white light by mixing just two colors of light together. Two colors of light that, when mixed together, make white light are called *complementary colors*. For example:

• red light plus green light makes white light
• violet light plus yellow light makes white light
• blue light plus orange light makes white light

It is also true that:

• white light minus green light makes red light
• white light minus yellow light makes violet light
• white light minus orange light makes blue light

This helps us understand what happened with the pictures we saw. When you stared at the green and yellow bell for a long time, the part of the eye that sees color got tired of seeing green and yellow and started to see these colors less well. When you quickly moved your eyes to the white paper, your eyes were too tired to see green and yellow in the white light. They could only see the colors that were left: the red and violet light.

• AFTER THE BELL •

Description of Drawing	Description of After-Image

ANALYSIS SHEET

31. LENSES

Topic • Optics

Materials • For each group of two or three students: one clear glass jar or bottle with a tight-fitting lid. They can be of varying sizes. Number the lid on each one so that it will be easier for students to talk about them. Each jar or bottle must be completely filled with water. This can be done before class or during class. Fill each jar with water and then let more water drip into it. Put the cap on and turn the jar sideways to be sure that there are no air bubbles. Be sure the caps are on tight. You will also need some small items for the students to examine with the bottle "lenses."

Demonstration

1. Show the students the jars, and ask them to guess what they could be used for. Elicit that they are used as lenses.

2. Divide the students into groups and pass out the jars and the small items. Tell the students to hold the jars and look at the items through them. What happens to the items? Suggest that they hold the jars different ways (horizontally and vertically) and at differing distances from the paper. How do the images change?

3. Encourage groups to exchange bottles and see how the images differ.

Analysis • Have each group use two different jars and draw what they see through the lenses as accurately as possible.

Application • Have the students, working in groups, make a list of all the lenses they can think of. What are they used for? Do they all make things bigger? The groups can all contribute to a list on the board or, more elaborately, make posters or large pictures for display.

Explanation • You see things because light rays come off of them. These light rays land on a group of nerve cells in the back of your eye, called the *retina*. When you look at something, you get an idea of its size from the amount of space the light rays from it take up on your retina. The more space they take up, the larger the object looks.

When you looked through the jar filled with water, you were looking through a magnifying **lens**. It magnifies or makes the object look bigger because it changes the path of the light rays going from the object to your eye. It makes the light rays take up more space on your retina.

The curve of a lens changes the path of the light. Because your lens curves only in one direction, around the jar, it magnifies in only one direction.

32. COLORED WATER/ COLORED AIR

Topic • Optics

Materials • A clear glass fishbowl or other deep glass bowl filled with water, 2 table-

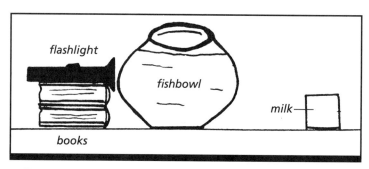

spoons of milk, a flashlight, two thick books, color photographs of sunsets in a variety of places (magazines are a good source).

Demonstration

1. Show the students the materials and talk about what they are. Darken the room. Put the flashlight on top of the books with the light shining through the water-filled bowl. Have the students observe the light from various angles and tell what they see. Ask them to try to guess if it will look different when milk is added to the water.

2. Have a volunteer stir half the milk into the water. Darken the room. Shine the flashlight beam at the bowl. Again have the students look at the light from various angles, including having the light shine over their shoulders and toward them. As they do this, have them tell what they see.

3. Add the remainder of the milk and again have the students observe the bowl from various angles.

Analysis • With the students' assistance, make a chart on the board with the phrases *plain water, water + 1 tablespoon of milk and water with 2 tablespoons of milk* down the side. Have the students help describe the different angles from which they viewed the light (e.g., from behind, from in front) and write those across the top. Record the observations in the chart. Discuss these questions: *Does the water change its color? How does the position of the light change the color you see?*

Application • Look at the pictures of sunsets with the students. Talk about the colors they see. Encourage them to talk about sunsets they have seen. Divide the students into small groups. Give them the following information and ask them to use what they have just learned to answer these questions: *Why is the sky a different color at sunrise and sunset than it is at noon? Why are some of the most beautiful sunsets in places where there is a lot of dust in the air?*

Explanation • When the demonstration started, there was only water in the bowl. When the light from the flashlight passed through it, the color of the water did not seem to change. When small bits of milk were added to the water, the light *scattered*, or broke up, just as the ocean's waves break up when they hit rocks. Different colors of light have different sized waves. Red light is made of big waves, but blue light has much smaller waves. The particles of milk scatter the blue part of the light when it shines through the side of the bowl. As a result, we see the color blue. It takes more particles to scatter red light. When there is more milk and we see the light through the whole bowl of water, the red part of the light is scattered, so the water looks pink.

The earth is covered with a blanket of air. The air is full of bits of dust and small drops of water. Like the milk in the bowl, the dust and water drops scatter the blue part of sunlight. This makes the sky look blue. When the sun is low in the sky, sunlight passes through a thicker layer of air, which scatters the red part of light. This makes the sky look pink or red.

33. BENDING LIGHT

Topic • Optics

Materials • For each group of four students: a glass filled with water, a straw, a coin, a bowl or cup, a container of water, copy of the Bending Light Directions.

Demonstration

1. Show the students the materials for the demonstrations. Tell them that they are going to see light bend. Give examples of *bend* if necessary. Explain that in one part of the demonstration they will put the straw in the water and observe what it looks like.

2. Divide the students into groups of four. All four can work on the same demonstration, or they can work in pairs on different ones. Give each group the materials and the directions. Be sure that each student draws and takes notes on her observations.

Analysis • Mix the students so they are in different groups. Have them compare the drawings and notes they made.

Application • *You and your friend are spear fishing from the shore of a pond. You see a fish near the surface. Your friend jabs his spear right at it, but he misses and the fish swims away. Now it's your turn. Here comes another fish. How will you aim your spear? Right at the fish? Above the fish? Below the fish? Why?* (Answer: In order to compensate for the refraction of the light rays, the successful fisherman must aim below where he sees the fish.)

Explanation • Light travels at different speeds through different materials. It travels more slowly through water or glass than it does through air. As the light slows down, it also changes direction a little. This is called **refraction**. Refraction makes the light waves look as if they bend. When you looked at the straw in the glass of water, part of it was above the water (in the air) and part of it was under the water. At the point where the air and water meet, the straw appears to bend. If you look at your arm or leg when you are in the bathtub or in a swimming pool, you will see the same effect.

When looking at the coin in the water, moving away from the container meant you could no longer see the coin. When you added water, the light from the coin was refracted, or bent, so that you could see the coin again. The coin looked as if it were higher than it really was.

• BENDING LIGHT •

DIRECTIONS

Straw in Water

Place the straw in the glass of water. Look down at the straw. Is the straw straight or does it bend? Take it out of the water. How does it look now? Draw a picture of what you actually see.

Coin in Water

Put the bowl or cup on the table. Put the coin in the bottom of it. Keep looking at the coin and move backward slowly until the coin disappears. Stay in the same place and ask your partner to pour water into the cup or bowl. What happens? Pour the water back into its original container and let your partner try it. When could you see the coin the second time? What made it possible for you to see it when there was water in the dish but not when there was no water? Make notes about what happens at each stage.

34. LIQUID LIGHT

Topic • Optics

Materials • A 2-liter clear plastic soft drink bottle, a sharp tool to make a hole in the bottle (ice pick, screwdriver, etc.), water, a flashlight, a bowl to catch the water as it pours

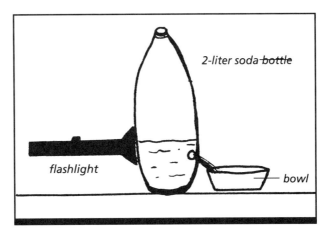

out. You will need to do the demonstration where all of the students can observe it.

Demonstration

1. Introduce the materials.

2. Make a hole in the bottle.

3. Have a volunteer cover the hole with her finger while a second volunteer fills the bottle to a level above the hole.

4. Place the lighted flashlight behind the bottle, pointing toward the hole. Turn off the lights.

5. Have the student who is covering the hole let go so the water will pour out.

Analysis • Divide the students into groups to share their observations and to decide how best to describe them. They may want to use the chalkboard or paper to draw what they observed. Have each group show and explain their observations. The demonstration can be repeated if the students are interested in seeing it again.

Application • Present the following information to the students. You may want to use it as a partial dictation for more advanced students or use a labeled drawing for less advanced students. Afterwards, ask them to tell you how it is related to the demonstration.

Have you ever wondered how doctors can study the organs inside your body? One way is by operating on a person, but this can be dangerous because it can further weaken a patient. It also can increase the chance of infection. Another way is by using X-rays, but these can also be dangerous to people. A third way, called an endoscope, uses the principle of total internal reflection which we saw in the demonstration. Very thin rods of glass are enclosed in a tube. The tube is put into the patient's body. Light is sent through the tube. No matter how the tube twists or turns, the light follows it. The doctor can see through it to look at the inside of the patient's body. Operations can even be done using this kind of equipment.

Explanation • When light goes from water into air, some of it is reflected and some of it gets through. How much gets reflected depends on the angle of the light. If the angle is small, some light gets through and some is reflected. But if the angle is big, all of the light is reflected. This is called *total internal reflection.* when you let the water run out of the bottle, the light from the flashlight followed the path of the water. This is an example of total internal reflection.

35. A HOLE IN THE HAND

Topic • Binocular vision

Materials • A sheet of paper for each student, pictures of animals.

Demonstration

1. Ask the students to roll the paper into a narrow tube.

2. Tell them to keep both eyes open and to hold the tube up to their left eyes. Because people have right or left eye preferences (dominant eye), some of your students will feel more comfortable looking through the tube with their right eyes.

3. Then ask them to place their right hands (left hands for those using their right eyes) up next to the tube, about two inches from the end. They will see a round hole through their hands.

Analysis • Ask your students if they all managed to see through their hands. If not, get those who were successful to help the others by making suggestions. Then ask them to consider the following questions: *Where is the best place to put your hand? Near the tube? Away from the tube? Touching the tube? What happens if you place your hand past the end of the tube? What happens if you bring your hand very close to your face? To look through the tube, which eye do you prefer, your left eye or your right eye?*

Application • With the class, look at some pictures of different animals. Have them notice the position of the eyes on various animals and ask them to guess the reasons for the differences. Provide the following information on animal vision if it has not come out of the discussion:

Because your eyes are a small distance apart, each eye sees a different view of the world. This helps you to see the shapes of objects and living things. It also helps you to determine how far away things are.

Most predators (animals that hunt)* have two eyes facing forward. Some examples of animal hunters are tigers, wolves, and eagles. These animals can see objects and judge distances very well, but they have a narrow view.

Other animals, such as rabbits, squirrels, and some fish, have eyes facing sideways. They have a wide view to help them look out for the hunters.

Provide the students with pictures of animals. Then have each student work with a partner to make a list of animals with eyes facing forward and animals with eyes facing sideways.

Explanation • When you look at something, your brain always combines the information from your two eyes to produce one picture. In this demonstration, each eye saw something different. One eye saw the circle made by the tube. The other eye saw your hand. Your brain combined what one eye saw through the tube with what the other eye saw: your hand. So you saw a picture of your hand with a hole through it!

*If your students have done Lesson 4, Animal Tracks, you may want to review that discussion of predators and prey.

36. THE BIRD IN THE CAGE

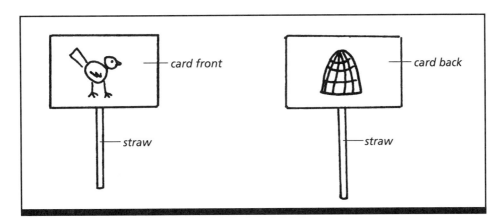

card front — straw

card back — straw

Topic • Optical illusion

Materials • Each student and the teacher will need one 3" × 5" index card, 1 straw, markers or crayons, and scissors. For the teacher's model, draw a bird on one side of the card and a bird cage on the other (see picture). Cut a ½ inch slit at one end of the straw so that it will hold the card.

Demonstration

1. Before class make a card as shown in the illustration, with a bird on one side and a cage on the other. Mount it on the straw.

2. Show the model to the students, pointing out the bird on one side and the cage on the other. Ask the students if they think you can put the bird in the cage. Have a show of hands of those who think you can do it. Ask volunteers to try it. If none of the students can do it, show them. Spin the straw by placing it between the palms of your hands, rubbing them back and forth. Ask the students to tell you what they observed.

3. Tell the students that they will each make their own cards by drawing a picture of a bird and a cage, a fish and a fishbowl, or a similar set of pictures. Ask the students to share their ideas for pictures. Tell them that the only limitations (aside from those of taste) are that both objects must be about the same size and be drawn in the middle of the card.

4. Pass out the materials. As students finish their pictures instruct them to make a slit at one end of the straw to hold the card, then to try the demonstration themselves by spinning the straw.

Analysis • Have the students share their cards with their classmates. As they do so, encourage them to talk about their pictures. Do all of the pictures work as their designers intended? If not, what went wrong?

Application • Discuss animated cartoons with your students. Which ones do they like? How are they made? Give them the following information:

Every time you see an animated cartoon you are seeing a series of pictures. In each picture, there is a slight change to show a character running, walking, talking or doing anything else the artist wants. When the pictures are put together and moved rapidly, the character appears to be moving.

Now instruct the students to make their own "moving picture" books, as described here

First get some paper ready. Decide how many pages you want. Cut pieces of paper into eight parts, making enough pages for your book. Cut them first in half lengthwise and then in fourths horizontally. Next, decide what you want to draw. Then draw a series of pictures. Finally, staple them together and flip through them to see them move.

Explanation • When you spun the card, the two pictures seemed to become one picture. This is called an *optical illusion*, which means that your eyes trick you into seeing something that is not really there. This kind of optical illusion happens because one picture or image stays in your vision for a fraction of a second after the picture is gone. When you spin the card rapidly, the new image appears before the old one is gone. The same principle applies when you flip rapidly through a series of pictures.

Sound

37. WHERE'S THE SOUND?

Topic • Location of sound

Materials • One copy of the Where's the Sound? Data Sheet for each student.

Demonstration

1. Tell the students that you are going to conduct an activity to find out if two ears are better than one. Hand out the data sheets.

2. Choose six students to stand in different locations around the room: two in the back of the room, one on the left and the other on the right; two halfway back in the room, one on the left and one on the right; and two in the front, one on the left and one on the right. Look at the data sheet and identify the student in each location.

3. Tell the remaining students to cover their eyes and to try to identify which of the six students is clapping. Point to one of the students who is standing. That student will clap once. Tell the students who are seated to point in the direction of the clap and then to circle the appropriate answer for the first clap on the data sheet.

4. Repeat this process, with each of the other five students clapping once, one at a time. (Note: Be sure to keep track of which student does each clap, in order to check student responses.)

5. Go over the responses with the students. Did everyone have the same answer?

6. Explain to the students that you are going to repeat the activity, but this time you are going to make it more interesting by having them cover their left ears as well as their eyes.

7. Repeat the activity, again pointing to students after the listeners' eyes are covered and having the students record their responses. Check the responses after all the claps.

Analysis • Have the students get together in groups of four and compare their data sheets. What generalizations can they make about the demonstration? How did their results differ when they listened with one ear and with two? Did their one-ear results differ depending on the direction of the clap?

Application • Divide the students into groups to brainstorm as many circumstances as they can think of in which it is essential for people or animals to identify the direction from which a sound comes. Then have them, either working in pairs or individually, make up stories describing such a circumstance. Alternatively, the students could draw pictures rather than write stories and present their pictures to the class.

Explanation • The clapping sound hits the ear nearest the sound a bit sooner and a bit louder than it hits the other ear. This gives your brain a clue about the direction from which it comes.

Name_____

• WHERE'S THE SOUND? •

Using both ears:

1st clap:

Right side   Left side   Back right   Back left   Front right   Front left

2nd clap:

Right side   Left side   Back right   Back left   Front right   Front left

3rd clap:

Right side   Left side   Back right   Back left   Front right   Front left

4th clap:

Right side   Left side   Back right   Back left   Front right   Front left

5th clap:

Right side   Left side   Back right   Back left   Front right   Front left

6th clap:

Right side   Left side   Back right   Back left   Front right   Front left

Number Correct: _____

Cover left ear:

1st clap:

Right side   Left side   Back right   Back left   Front right   Front left

2nd clap:

Right side   Left side   Back right   Back left   Front right   Front left

3rd clap:

Right side   Left side   Back right   Back left   Front right   Front left

4th clap:

Right side   Left side   Back right   Back left   Front right   Front left

5th clap:

Right side   Left side   Back right   Back left   Front right   Front left

6th clap:

Right side   Left side   Back right   Back left   Front right   Front left

Number Correct: _____

DATA SHEET

38. WE'RE ALL EARS

Topic • Focusing sound

Materials • For each pair of students: a paper cup, a tube (empty paper towel or toilet paper roll), sheets of paper, tape, scissors, animal pictures. (Students may be responsible for bringing them in; animal pictures from Lesson 35, A Hole in the Hand, may be used.)

Demonstration

1. Divide the students into pairs and give them the materials. Then tell them that they have 15 minutes to use the materials provided to make something that will help them hear better.

2. Ask them to try out their devices by listening to a whispered message with and without the help of the device.

3. When they have all done this, put pairs together to make groups of four. Ask them to try out both of the devices and to decide which one enhances their hearing the most.

Analysis • Draw a picture of the device you chose. Why/How does it work? Try to design an even better one.

Application • Collect pictures of animals with different kinds of ears. Then cut off all the ears and stick them all on a piece of paper. Stick the pictures of the animals minus their ears on separate sheets of paper. Staple the sheets together into a book. Ask your classmates to match the animals with their ears. For each animal, consider: In which direction do they hear best? Why?

Explanation • The best kind of device probably has much the same shape as the human ear or a funnel. The outer part of the funnel serves to catch the sound/vibration while the tube carries it directly to the eardrum. An old-fashioned kind of hearing aid was called an *ear trumpet*. The small end was put in the ear while the large end was held toward the speaker.

39. COAT HANGER CHIMES

Topic • Vibrations

Materials • For the initial presentation, a rubber band. For each pair of students: two pencils with eraser ends, a 36-inch length of string, a metal coat hanger, different-ent sized metal spoons.

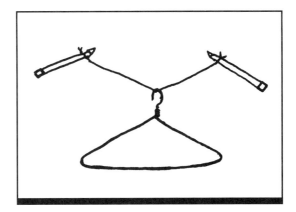

Demonstration

1. Begin by writing the term **vibration** on the board. Ask the students to put their hands on their throats and to say a short word. (*Oh* is a good one.) What do the students feel? Their vocal cords are vibrating. Ask a student to hold a rubber band taut between her hands. Have another student pluck it. What happens? This time the students can see the rubber band's vibrations. Now get the students to formulate a definition of *vibration*. Can they think of other examples?

2. Show the students the materials. Ask them what kinds of sounds they could make with those materials.

3. Divide the class into pairs and hand out the materials.

4. Tell the students to tie the string to the hook of the coat hanger so that there is an equal amount of string on either side.

5. Have the students tie a pencil by the writing end to each end of the string.

6. Now instruct one of the students in each pair to place the eraser ends of the pencils in his ears and, while holding them there, to swing the hanger against the table or desk.

7. Have the other partner do the same.

Analysis • Ask the students to describe the sound they heard. Encourage them to compare it with a sound they know (chimes, for example). Then ask them to try to tell you how the sound was produced and how it reached their ears.

Application • Tell the students that chimes can be made by using a metal spoon instead of a coat hanger. Give each pair at least two different sizes of spoons and encourage them to experiment by attaching the string to the handles of the spoons and listening through the pencil ends while they hit the spoon against a desk. What differences in sound do they observe? What causes the differences? Why?

Explanation • When the coat hanger hits a table or other solid object, it vibrates. This was the source of the sound you heard during the demonstration. These vibrations are called *sound waves*. Sound waves travel more easily through solid objects than through the air. The vibrations you heard traveled through the metal coat hanger, then through the string and the pencils to your ear drum. The vibrations of the pencil were transferred to your ear drum, which made it possible for you to hear the chiming sound.

40. CANNED MESSAGES

Topic • Sound waves

Materials • Each pair of students will need two empty cans without tops (paper cups may be substituted), a long piece of string, and one copy of the Canned Messages Student Directions.

Demonstration

1. Before class make a hole in the bottom of each can using a hammer and a nail.

2. Ask the students if they think they can hear a whisper from one end of the class to the other. Then have several pairs of students try it. Tell them that today they are going to make a device that will make it easy for them to do this. Show them the materials and ask them to predict what they are going to make.

3. Divide them into pairs and give each pair a set of materials plus the student directions.

4. When they have made the can telephones, have each pair then try to send messages to each other from one end of the room to the other.

Analysis • Ask the students to consider the following questions: *How does the sound travel from one can to the other? What happens if the string is not tight? Why? Does sound travel faster through solids or through gases? Why is the answer to the last question important in this activity?*

Application • Draw the following picture of a can telephone on an overhead. Have the students write down all the things that are

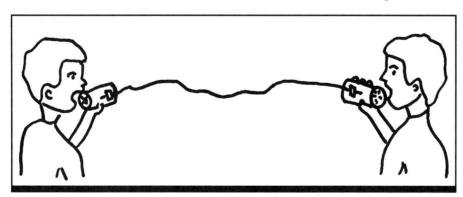

wrong with it (e.g., the string is not tight, both people have the cans to their mouths).

Explanation • When you speak into the can you make the air inside vibrate. This makes the bottom of the can vibrate. These vibrations travel down the taut string and cause the bottom of the other can and the air inside it to vibrate. These vibrations are then passed along to the ear.

• CANNED MESSAGES •

1. Put the end of the piece of string through the hole in the bottom of one of the cans.

2. Tie a knot in the string. This will stop the string from slipping back through the hole.

3. Repeat the process with the other end of the string and the other can.

4. Your can telephone is now ready. Each partner should take one of the cans and move away from each other until the string is stretched tightly. Take turns speaking and listening.

41. SCRATCHING THE SURFACE

Topic • Vibrations

Materials • A wooden table or desk

Demonstration

1. Ask pairs of students to sit with a table or desk between them. Tell the students that you're going to see how sensitive their hearing is. Then scratch your own desk and ask them if they can hear the sound. Start as softly as possible and gradually increase in intensity until most students indicate they can hear it. Encourage them to speculate on why some students heard the sound before others.

2. Have the students work in pairs with one student scratching the desk and the other student listening.

3. Then ask the listening students to put their ears flat down on the desk while they listen again. Have the student report what happens.

4. Get the students to exchange roles and repeat the procedure.

Analysis • Ask the students to consider these questions in groups: *Why did some students hear the sound before others when the teacher scratched the desk? Why did the scratching sound louder when the listeners put their ears flat down on the desk?*

Application • Put the following words on the board: *desert, escape, ground, ear.* Tell the students that there is a story that links these items and their job is to find it. They can ask you "yes/no" questions until they find the story. Here is one possible story. You may invent your own.

A man is lost in the desert without food. He puts his ear to the ground and can hear cars on a road five miles away. He makes his way to the road and is saved.

Explanation • Students nearer to the teacher's desk heard the scratching sound more easily than those students sitting farther away. This is because sound is carried by sound waves. As you get farther away from the source of the sound, the waves get smaller. This is the same as when you throw a rock in a pool of water. The waves closest to the rock are the biggest and those which are farther away are smaller. Big waves cause loud sounds, and small waves cause soft sounds.

The scratching sound is louder when you have your ear to the desk because sound waves travel more easily through solids than through gases. Wood is a solid and air is a gas. When your ear is away from the desk, the sound waves have to travel through air to reach it, but when your ear is on the desk, the waves only have to travel through wood.

42. ECHO... ECHO... ECHO...

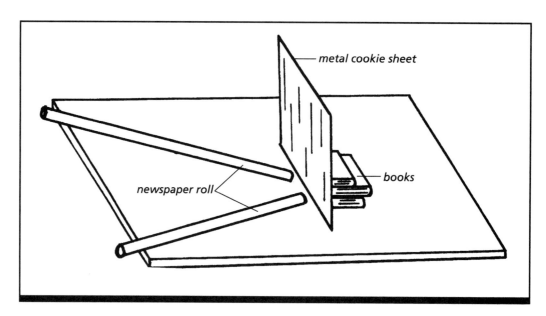

metal cookie sheet

newspaper roll

books

Topic • Echoes

Materials • Three sheets of newspaper for each student. For each pair of students: a desk or table, a large flat metal cookie baking sheet, a towel, masking tape.

Demonstration

1. Give each student three sheets of newspaper. Have them roll the three sheets together into a tube with a 1½ inch diameter (approximately) and use masking tape to hold the tube firmly together.

2. Divide the students into pairs and give each pair a cookie sheet.

3. Direct each pair to make the cookie sheet stand up on the far edge of the desk. This can be done by leaning the sheet against the wall or by propping it up with books.

4. Next ask them to put the newspaper tubes on the desk as shown in the diagram. It is important that they are both at the same angle to the cookie sheet.

5. Ask one of the pair to whistle or whisper into one of the tubes while the other listens with his ear as close to the second tube as possible. Have them change roles.

6. Tell the students to cover the cookie sheet with the towel and try the demonstration again. What happens?

Analysis • Answer the following questions together: *Can you hear the whistle/whisper distinctly through the tube? How does the sound travel from one tube to the other? How did the towel affect the sound?*

Application • Ask groups of students to find out how each of the following use echoes:

bats   submarines   whales   fishermen   doctors

Explanation • The sound does not come directly from one tube to the other. It reflects off the cookie sheet in the same way light is reflected by a mirror. Sound always reflects off hard surfaces, but often we don't hear it, either because the vibrations spread out in all directions and get lost, or because there is so little time between the original sound and the echo that the human ear can't tell the two apart. This happens if we are standing closer than 50 feet to the reflecting surface. In caves and tunnels, the reflected sounds are trapped so we can hear them more clearly. In addition, they may be reflected more than once so that there is a greater time delay between the original sound and the later reflections. When you covered the cookie sheet with the towel, the sound was no longer reflected. It was absorbed by the towel.

43. DRUM BEAT

Topic • Vibrations

Materials • For the first activity: a metal bowl, a large saucepan, a large spoon, a piece of plastic wrap slightly larger than the bowl, a large rubber band, a few grains of rice. For the second activity: a variety of sizes of saucepans and spoons.

Demonstration

1. Choose two students and read the following directions to them while the rest of the class watches to see if the two students are carrying out the directions correctly: *Cover the top of the metal bowl with the plastic wrap. Use the rubber band to keep the plastic firmly in place. Pull the plastic down on both sides to stretch it very tightly.*

2. Ask the other students what they think it looks like and what it is going to be used for.

3. Ask the selected students to spread a few grains of rice on the surface of the plastic.

4. Ask the rest of the students again what they think it is going to be used for.

5. Give a different student the saucepan and the spoon and ask her to stand close to the bowl without touching it. Then ask her to hit the bottom of the saucepan as hard as possible with the spoon while the other students watch the rice.

Analysis • Ask the students to consider the following questions: *What did the rice do? What caused it? How?* Then let them take turns experimenting to find out the answers to these questions: *What happens if you use a smaller saucepan? What happens if you use a smaller spoon? What happens if you strike the saucepan farther away from the bowl?*

Application • Some birds find worms and insects under the ground through vibrations. How do you think they do this?

Explanation • When the spoon hits the saucepan it causes the air to vibrate violently and this produces a noise. The vibrations move through the air and cause the tightly stretched plastic film to vibrate too, which in turn makes the rice move. If a smaller spoon or saucepan is used, the air is less disturbed and the vibrations are less violent. Therefore, they may not move the rice. As the vibrations travel, they become less violent and again may not disturb the rice.

This is very similar to the human eardrum. Vibrations or sound waves cause the eardrum to vibrate and these vibrations move through the middle ear to the inner ear. In the inner ear they are changed into electrical messages. The brain interprets these electrical messages as sounds.

Sound waves can move through solids and liquids as well as through air. You can hear a friend make a noise under water when you are swimming. You can feel the vibrations from loud music through your feet as well as through your ears.

44. ELASTIC GUITAR

Topic • Vibrations

Materials • For each pair of students: an empty tissue box (a shoe box may also be used if you cut a hole in the lid), five rubber bands of different lengths and widths, two pencils.

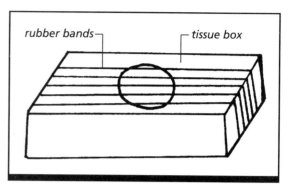

Demonstration

1. Give each student a rubber band and let him experiment to see what notes he can make by plucking it. Ask the students to suggest ways they could improve the sound. Ask them if it makes any difference how much they stretch the band or how long it is.

2. Give the remaining materials to students in pairs, and instruct them to make a guitar by stretching the five rubber bands across the top of the box as in the picture. Ask them to pluck the bands and to report back how the notes sound.

3. Then ask them to insert the pencils between the box and the rubber bands so that the bands are no longer resting directly on the box. Does this improve the sound?

4. Finally ask them to try to pick out a tune.

Analysis • Have the students consider these questions in groups and report back to the class: *Which bands give the highest notes? Why? Which bands give the lowest notes? Why? What happens if you tighten the bands? Why? What did adding the pencils do to improve the sound?*

Application • Make a list of musical instruments that use a box to amplify their sound. What kind of material is the box usually made of? Why? Which other instruments use strings? How does a piano work? If you have access to stringed instruments, bring them to class and let the students try playing them.

Explanation • If a string or band vibrates very fast it will have a high sound. If it vibrates more slowly it will make a lower sound. Strings can vibrate very fast if they are thin, short, and tight; they vibrate more slowly if they are thick, long, and loose. Thin, short, tight strings make the highest notes.

If the rubber bands are resting directly against the box when they start to vibrate, they hit the side of the box; this limits the vibration. The sound improves when you use the pencils to hold the rubber bands away from the top of the box because the bands can then vibrate freely.

45. NOISEMAKERS

Topic • Vibrations

Materials • A balloon for each student; for each pair of students: a straw, a pair of scissors, a 2-inch square of cellophane, a comb, and a piece of tissue paper.

Demonstration

1. Show the students the balloons and ask them how you can make a noise using a balloon.

2. Give each student a balloon and have a competition to see who can make the most noise using them. You may want to do this outside on a nice day. Let the students take turns making their noise and have all the students judge who made the most noise.

3. Have the student who made the most noise explain exactly what he did.

4. Have the students experiment to see how many different sounds they can make.

Analysis • In groups, list changes you can make in the balloon which will change the noise produced.

Application • Put the students in pairs and give them the remaining materials. Encourage them to make as many different noises as possible using them. Ask them to list how many noises they were able to make and how they made them. Some suggestions:

1. The comb and tissue can be used to make a kazoo.

2. The straw can be cut into a point at one end. If you blow through this end, the straw vibrates like the reed in some musical instruments.

3. If you hold the cellophane up in front of your mouth and blow with your lips together on the edge, it will produce a very loud noise. Blowing makes the thin piece of cellophane vibrate very quickly.

Explanation • As the air comes out of the balloon it makes the neck of the balloon vibrate. This produces a "raspberry" noise. The amount of air in the balloon, plus the size and shape of the hole it escapes through, all change the noise produced. If there is a lot of air in the balloon it will be under more pressure, and this will cause the neck of the balloon to vibrate more and make more noise. If the hole the air escapes through is kept very small, this will also increase the pressure and therefore produce more noise.

Follow-up • You may want to show the students wind instruments or pictures of them and talk about how they work. Encourage the students to find similarities between their noisemakers and the instruments.

PROPERTIES OF LIQUIDS

46. HEAPING PENNIES

Topic • Surface tension

Note • This lesson can be used immediately before Lesson 47, Liquid Trails.

Materials • For each pair of students: a penny, an eyedropper (available in a drugstore or hobby shop), a small container of water.

Demonstration

1. Show the students the materials. Ask them to predict how many drops of water a penny will hold. Write their predictions on the chalkboard.

2. Divide the students into pairs and hand out the materials. Have the students decide which person will drop the water and which one will count the drops. Have them drop water on the penny until the water spills off. They should record the number of drops.

3. Have the students dry off the penny and change roles. Again they will count and record the number of drops. Have each pair average the number of drops the penny holds.

Analysis • Make a chart of the results on the board or on a large piece of paper. How did the class predictions of the number of drops compare with the actual number of drops? What did the water on the penny look like when it had the most drops on it? What did it look like after that? Have student volunteers draw "before" and "after" pictures on the board.

Application • Divide the students into pairs. Ask them to try to imagine what it would be like if water were not cohesive. What would it be like to swim in it? To drink it? Would there be puddles after it rains? After the pairs discuss these questions, ask them to make up a story about the topic. Before the students begin to write, you may want to have some of the pairs tell some of the implications of not having cohesion.

Explanation • When drops of water are put on top of a penny, the drops stick together. This happens because the water molecules are attracted to each other. This "hold-together" force is called **cohesion**. The drops form one large drop of water on top of the penny because the surface of the water has a kind of skin called **surface tension**. Surface tension holds the water together in drops. As you add more drops to the penny, the weight of the water becomes too much and the surface tension breaks, spilling the water. You can reduce the surface tension of water by adding soap to it. This makes the water's skin stretch more. That is why you can blow bubbles with soapy water.

Follow-up • You may want to have the students try other liquids (one per group), such as cooking oil, soapy water, or alcohol, and report their findings.

47. LIQUID TRAILS

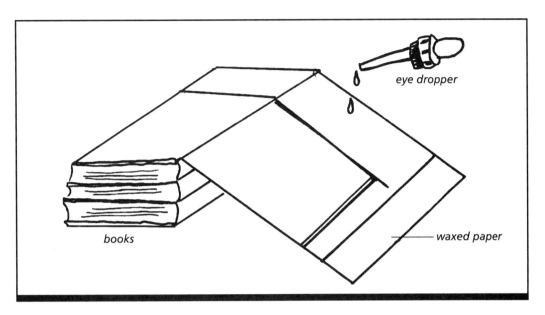

eye dropper

books

waxed paper

Topic • Adhesion

Materials • A 12" piece of waxed paper taped on a piece of cardboard or a baking sheet; small amounts of cooking oil, water, soapy water, and rubbing alcohol (the same liquids can be used in the Follow-up of Lesson 46, Heaping Pennies); an eye dropper for each liquid (available in drugstores or hobby shops); a small stack of books to make an incline; a piece of writing paper for each student.

Demonstration

1. Stack the books so that they will hold the mounted waxed paper on an incline. Set the waxed paper on the incline. Seat the students so they can all see the waxed paper.

2. Show the students the liquids and identify them. Dictate the names of the liquids to the students, having them write the names and leave a space after each on their writing paper. Explain that they will make notes of their observations.

3. Ask a volunteer to drop one of the liquids on the waxed paper near the high end, near one side. Tell the class to observe the trail that is left and to make a note of what they see.

4. Continue until all of the liquids have been used. Each liquid should be dropped an inch or more to one side of the others, so the different trails can be readily identified. Have volunteer students go to the board and draw the trails they observed.

Analysis • Ask the students to use their notes and pictures of the trails to tell what they observed. What did each trail look like? How were they different? Why were they different? What kind of trail would a drop of honey make?

Application • Have the students, working in groups, brainstorm as many ways as they can to stick a piece of paper to the wall.

Explanation • When you dropped the liquids on the waxed paper, you saw that each one left a different kind of trail. That is, some of the liquid was left behind, sticking to the waxed paper. The "sticking force" that held bits of the liquids to the waxed paper is called **adhesion**. Molecules in a liquid are not only attracted to each other (**cohesion**), but they are also attracted to other kinds of molecules (**adhesion**).

48. SOLUTIONS

Topic • Solubility

Materials • For each group: a small, clear plastic glass or cup half full of water, a flat toothpick, a teaspoon or two of powdered drink mix (such as Kool-Aid)—preferably of a dark color such as grape or cherry—which can be put on a small piece of waxed paper.

Demonstration

1. Divide the students into groups and distribute the materials. Ask the students if they have ever used the drink mix. What can they tell about it?

2. Direct the groups to have one person at a time in charge of adding drink mix to the water. They will do this by picking up a small amount of the drink mix on the wide end of the toothpick and gently shaking the powder over the water. Ask them to observe what happens from the side of the glass.

3. Have the students add more mix to the water and continue observing the results.

Analysis • Discuss these questions with the students: *What happened when the mix was dropped on the water? Did it all stay together at the top? In what direction did it move through the water? As more mix was added, what happened to the water? Can you see the mix? Can you see the water?*

Application • Have each student test five other materials at home to see if they will dissolve in water. Ask them to keep a record of the materials they tried and the results. When the students return with their results, divide them into groups. Give each group a large sheet of paper on which to record their results. Ask each group to present its results to the class. If possible, post the sheets around the classroom.

Explanation • The crystals of powdered drink mix **dissolve** in the water as they fall. When they dissolve, they break into smaller and smaller pieces and spread everywhere in the water. The mixture that results is called a **solution**. It will not separate, even if it stands for a long time. When you add sugar to coffee, you are making a solution. The sugar dissolves more quickly if the coffee is hot. If you put in too much sugar, not all of it will dissolve. The extra sugar will fall to the bottom.

49. WILL IT OR WON'T IT?

Topic • Buoyancy

Materials • A clear glass or plastic container; water; an assortment of objects such as a toothpick, an eraser, a cork, a small piece of wood, an apple, a bottle cap, a nail, a coin (be sure you have some objects that will sink and some that will float); a piece of writing paper for each student; for the Application, each group will need a piece of modeling clay.

Demonstration

1. Write the words *float* and *sink* on the board. Have the class explain what they mean. Show the objects to the class and write the objects' names as students give them. Have the students make a list of them on a piece of paper. After each word, have the students write *F* if they think the object will float and *S* if they think it will sink.

2. On the board, write the number of students who put *F* and *S* next to each word.

3. Have a volunteer put each object in the water as the rest of the class watches. Have another student record *F* or *S* on the board.

Analysis • Compare the guesses with the results. Which ones were surprising? Why did some objects float and others sink? What was similar about the objects that floated? About the objects that sank?

Application • Drop a ball of modeling clay in the water. Does it sink or float? Divide the class into groups of three or four. Give each group a piece of clay and direct them to reshape it so it will float. When every group is ready, have the groups tell about and demonstrate their designs.

Explanation • Why do some things float and others sink? When we put the objects in the water, we saw that some things that were big floated, while some that were small sank. Some heavy objects floated and others sank. We learned that size or weight alone did not tell us which objects would float and which would sink.

What do we need to know about an object if we want to predict if it will float or sink? We need to know two characteristics: **density** and **displacement**.

Density is how heavy something is for its size. If an object is less dense than water, the water will hold it up. If it is more dense than water, the water will not hold it up. At the same time, the shape of an object is important.

Displacement is the weight or volume of a fluid displaced by a floating object. When an object floats in water, it moves some water out of the way. The water pushes back. The amount of push from the water depends on the amount of water the object **displaces**. You may have noticed the water level go up in the container when you put objects in the water. The water level went up because water was displaced by the objects. If the amount of water that an object displaces weighs more than the object does, the object will float. If it weighs less, the object will sink.

50. FLOATING COLORS

Topic • Density

Materials • A tall, slender clear glass container, such as a vase or a glass; equal amounts of corn syrup, water, cooking oil, and (denatured) rubbing alcohol; three different bottles of food coloring.

layered liquids

Demonstration

1. Show the students the liquids. Ask them to identify each one by smell or feel and to tell what it is used for. Have them make a list of the liquids on a piece of paper. Tell them that you are going to put all the liquids in the glass together. Ask them to guess which will be on top, on the bottom, etc. and to write a number after each one indicating the order, starting with #1 at the bottom. Summarize the predictions on the board, eliciting reasons as you write down numbers.

2. Add food coloring to the corn syrup and pour it in the container. Ask a student to describe it as you pour it. Ask the students to predict what will happen when you add the water. Put a different color in the water. Then add the water to the corn syrup, pouring it gently down the side of the container. Ask the students to describe what they see. Do the same with the oil and the alcohol (but do not add color to the alcohol), again asking students to predict and describe what happens.

Analysis • Compare the actual order of the layers of liquid with the students' predictions.

Application • Present the following information to your students:

From time to time, because of accidents to ships or oil wells, oil spills into the sea. The largest oil spill in the history of the United States came from the oil tanker, Valdez, in March 1989 in Alaska. Millions of gallons of crude oil spilled into the sea, causing widespread shore damage as well. Look in your school library for information about that or other oil spills. How do people clean up the oil? Does the information you have learned from this demonstration help you understand both the kinds of damage caused by oil spills and the ways they clean them up?

Explanation • When you poured the liquids into the glass, each one floated on the one underneath it. This happened because of the density of the liquids. Density means how much a certain volume of a material weighs. The density of a liquid depends on the size and number of molecules. One material floats on top of another because it has less density. The four liquids in this demonstration all had different densities. Oil and vinegar salad dressing is another example of liquids with different densities.

Note • In lieu of (or in addition to) the written explanation, you may want to try this technique: Make a square piece of paper to represent each liquid. For the densest one, corn syrup, put a lot of dots close together. The dots represent the molecules in the liquid. For each liquid in order of decreasing density put fewer dots. Have the students put them in order. This gives them a sense of what differing densities means.*

*I learned this technique from a presentation by Cecilia Welborn and Kimberley Tidwell of Burlington North Carolina

51. FLOATING EGGS

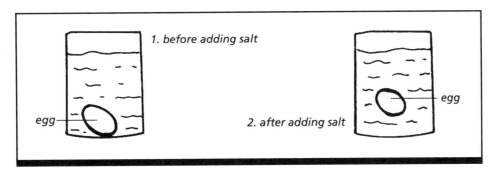

1. before adding salt

egg

2. after adding salt

egg

Topic • Buoyancy

Materials • A glass saucepan or other clear container of water, a fresh egg, salt, a tablespoon, copies of the Floating Eggs Application Sheet; for the Follow-up: other substances, such as sugar, baking soda, or corn syrup that will dissolve in water.

Demonstration

1. Introduce the materials. Put the words *float* and *sink* on the board. Ask the students to predict what will happen if you put the egg in the water. Will it float or sink?

2. Ask one of the students to put the egg in the water. What happens?

3. Ask the students if they know of any way to change the water so that the egg will float.

4. Have a volunteer put three tablespoons of salt in the container and stir it. What happens to the egg?

5. Ask a student to add more fresh water to the container. What happens?

Analysis • Either as a class or in small groups, ask the students to recount what happened. Have them answer and discuss the following questions: *Why does the egg sink in fresh water? Why does the egg float in salt water? What happens when you decrease the amount of salt by adding more fresh water?*

Application • Have your students read the information and instructions on the application sheet. If you have done Lesson 26,

Make a Compass, you may want to have them review what they learned about directions and use that to describe the locations of the lakes mentioned.

After the students write their stories, they may want to share them in pairs or with the whole class.

Explanation • The egg sank when we put it in fresh water. Objects can float only if their **density** is less than the density of the liquid they are in. **Density** means how heavy something is for its size. The density of the egg was more than the density of the fresh water. When we added salt to the water we increased its density. The salt water was denser than the egg, so the egg floated in it. For the same reason, fresh water will stay on top of salt water.

Follow-up • Bring other substances such as sugar, baking soda, or corn syrup to dissolve in water. As the students try floating the egg in these other substances, keep a chart of the results. Encourage the students to guess in advance what will happen and to explain why. Ask the students to describe what happens as they experiment.

• FLOATING EGGS •

Salt Lakes

In various parts of the world you can find salt lakes. Tsinghai Lake in China, the Great Salt Lake in the United States, the Dead Sea on the border between Israel and Jordan, and the Caspian Sea, which is bordered by Russia, Azerbaijan, Kazakhstan, Turkmenistan, and Iran, are all lakes of this kind. Look at a world map and find each one.

1. Using what you have learned from this demonstration, do you think swimming in a salt lake would be different from swimming in a freshwater lake?

2. Imagine that you and your friends are on vacation at one of these lakes. Write a short story about your adventures.

52. BUBBLE BABIES

Topic • Buoyancy

Materials • Fresh grapes, a sharp knife (for peeling the grapes), a clear drinking glass, a clear carbonated soft drink, such as 7-Up or Sprite; for the Application: a copy of the Bubble Babies Application Sheet for each group or pair of students.

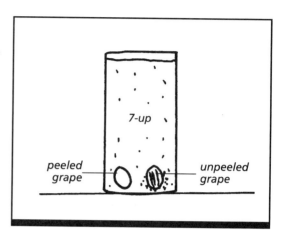

Demonstration

1. Take out two grapes. Peel one, leaving it whole.

2. Have student volunteers compare the weight of the two grapes in their hands and tell you which feels heavier. Have them describe the way the two grapes feel.

3. Ask a student to pour the soft drink into the glass. Have the students guess what you are going to do next. When someone guesses that you are going to put the grapes in the soft drink, ask them to speculate on whether they will both float.

4. Have a volunteer drop both grapes into the glass. Ask the class to observe what happens.

Analysis • Have each student draw a picture of the glass and the grapes when one grape is floating on top of the soft drink and the other is at the bottom of the glass. Have them identify the peeled and unpeeled grapes. Do the grapes look the same? Have the students compare their pictures with the picture at the top of the page when both grapes are at the bottom. Do the grapes look the same? What is different about them?

Application • Assign the students to pairs or small groups to work on the problem. Give each group or pair a copy of the application sheet. Students can report on their solutions orally or in writing.

They may want to draw pictures to accompany their reports. In order to successfully raise the treasure, their plans should include trapping air in the plastic, which is attached to the treasure by the rope.

Explanation • When you dropped the peeled grape into the glass, it sank to the bottom and stayed there. None of the bubbles from the soda could stick to it. When you dropped the unpeeled grape into the glass, it also dropped to the bottom. While it was at the bottom of the glass, some bubbles stuck to its skin. These bubbles are a gas called *carbon dioxide* or CO_2. They are lighter than the soda. When the bubbles stuck to the grape's skin, they made the grape bigger (increased its volume) but did not make it weigh much more.

   With the bubbles sticking to it, the **density** of the grape was less than that of the soda. Therefore, the grape went up to the surface. While it was on top, it lost some of the bubbles and sank to the bottom again. At the bottom, it picked up more bubbles.

Name_____

• BUBBLE BABIES •

Read the following problem with your group. Solve the problem. You will present your solution to your classmates.

Sunken Treasure

Imagine that you are a diver looking for treasure. One day while you are diving, you find a very old boat that is full of treasure. You want to get the boat and the treasure to the surface of the water so that you can see it better. You have the following equipment: a large piece of plastic, rope, and an air tank. What did you learn from this demonstration that would help you bring the boat and the treasure to the surface?

CHEMISTRY

53. ICE ON A THREAD

Topic • Melting point

Materials • A clear glass or plastic cup, cold water, an ice cube, a piece of thread, salt in a shaker; copy of the Ice on a Thread Analysis Sheet for each student.

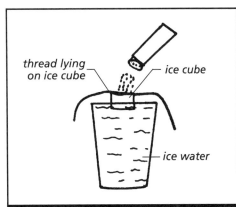

thread lying on ice cube — ice cube

ice water

Demonstration

1. Ask the students to tell you what they know about water and ice. You may want to make some notes on the board as they do so. Meanwhile, fill the cup with water and put the ice cube in it.

2. Ask the students to tell you how you could pick up the ice without touching it. Next show the students the thread. Ask them to suggest how you could use it to pick up the ice cube. Show them the salt shaker and ask how salt could help.

3. Place the thread on the ice cube and put salt on it, especially near the thread.

4. Wait a minute or so. Lift the thread slowly to see whether the water above it has frozen. If it has, lift both ends of the thread and the ice will come out of the water.

Analysis • Have the students write a step-by-step account of the demonstration on the analysis sheets, using the key words provided. Ask them to compare their papers in pairs and to make any corrections they think are needed.

Application • First ask the students to share their experiences with winter weather, ice, and snow. Then have them read or listen to the passage below. Finally, have students discuss the information and their answers to the questions.

In places where there is cold weather in the winter, the streets often become covered with ice and snow. They are slippery and dangerous. One way to make the streets safer is to melt the snow and ice by

putting salt on them. What is the effect of salt on the streets? If the temperature of the air is very, very cold, salt is not effective in melting ice. Why not?

Explanation • Every liquid has a certain temperature at which it freezes or melts. The freezing point of water is 32° F (0° C). When water gets below that temperature, it will freeze; when it gets above that temperature, it will melt. But salt water has a lower freezing temperature than plain water. In the demonstration, we began with an ice cube made from plain water. After we put the thread on the ice cube, we added salt. That changed the plain water around the thread to salt water. Because the freezing and melting point of salt water is lower than that of fresh water, the salty part of the ice cube melted. As the ice melted, the salt water was mixed with more plain water. This moved the freezing point back up toward 32°. Then the ice froze again, leaving the thread under the new ice. Because the thread was now frozen into the ice, we could lift the cube with it.

• ICE ON A THREAD •

Write a step-by-step description of the demonstration. Use the key words to help you.

1. (ice/water)

2. (thread/ice)

3. (salt/thread)

4. (ice/melt)

5. (ice/freeze)

6. (lift/ice)

ANALYSIS SHEET

54. SUPERBALLS

Topic • Chemical reaction

Materials • One superball, one box Twenty Mule Team Borax (available in the detergent section of the supermarket), Elmer's or other white glue, water; for each group: measuring cup, one quart container, mixing spoon, copy of the Superballs Student Sheet.

Demonstration

1. Hold up the superball. Ask the students if they know what kind of ball it is. After getting several responses, bounce the ball on the floor and observe how high it bounces. Repeat several times. Tell the students they are going to make a superball. Ask them if they have any ideas about what ingredients they will use.

2. Divide the class into groups of four. Hand out the student sheet. Have each group choose one person to collect the supplies the group will need.

Analysis • Have the students answer the questions on the student sheet. Then discuss them with the entire class. Can they think of other substances that change form when they are mixed together?

Application • Let the students have a contest with the balls they made to see which one will bounce the highest. Why do some bounce higher than others? Have the students make predictions based on the size and shape of the balls.

Explanation • When you mixed the Borax, water, and glue together, a *chemical reaction* occurred. In a chemical reaction, one or more substances are mixed together or combined in some way. When this happens, they form a new substance. The new substance is different from the chemicals that formed it.

Follow-up • Make instant pudding (mixes can be found in the supermarket) in class or suggest that the students make pudding as homework. What is similar about making pudding and making superballs?

• SUPERBALLS •

Superball Directions

1. To start, you will need $^1/_4$ cup of Borax and 2 cups of water.

2. Mix the Borax and the water. The solution should be cloudy. Some of the Borax will fall to the bottom of the container.

3. Add about 1 tablespoon of glue to the Borax and water.

4. Mix it all together with a spoon. The mixture should get very thick.

5. Squeeze out the extra water. Roll the material into a ball.

Analysis Questions

1. What was the mixture like before you added the glue?

2. What was it like after you added the glue?

3. How did the glue change the mixture?

STUDENT SHEET

55. WHAT COLOR IS IT?

Topic • Chromatography

Materials • For each group: a strip of blotting paper, paper towel, or coffee filter (2 inches wide by 5 inches long); a clear plastic cup with 1 to 2 inches of water in it; and a water-soluble marker (use a different color for each group). For the Application: the same materials listed above, plus different colors of food coloring.

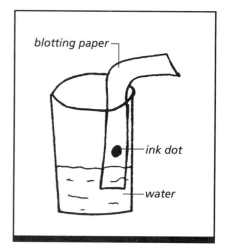

Demonstration

1. Before handing out the materials, have the students identify them. Ask them to tell you the colors of the markers. List the colors on the board.

2. Divide the class into groups of three or four and distribute the materials.

3. Tell the students to put a big, thick spot of ink from the group's marker on the blotting paper just above the water level in their cup. They can measure it from the outside of the cup. Then have them put the blotting paper inside the cup, with the ink above the water. They may want to prop the top end of the paper up against some books.

Analysis • Have the students make a list of the colors that appear on the paper. Next to each color listed on the board, list the colors the students report seeing on their blotters.

Application • The teacher and/or students take turns making "mystery mixes" using a few drops of two or three different food colors in water. They write the ingredients down separately without letting others see their papers. The other students then use blotting paper to try to identify the mixes and check their answers against the written list of ingredients.

Explanation • The colored inks in your markers are a mixture of a basic set of dyes, or coloring materials, in differing amounts. When you write with the pens, you only see one color. When you put the paper in the water, the paper **absorbed** the water. As this happened, the different dyes **dissolved** in the water. Some of these dyes dissolved more easily than others. As a result, they separated from each other. The rainbow pattern on your paper shows the dyes used to make the color you could see.

56. FIZZ!!

Topic • Chemical reaction

Materials • For each group: six clear plastic cups, vinegar (or lemon juice), water, two teaspoons, two tablespoons, baking powder, baking soda, two sheets of paper. For the Application: cake ingredients as listed on the Fizz!! Application Sheet.

Demonstration

1. Divide the class into groups. Distribute the materials to each group. Have each group fill one cup with water and fill the other half-way with vinegar. Two of the remaining empty cups should be placed on each sheet of paper. One piece of paper should be labeled *baking powder* and the cups marked *#1* and *#2*. The other piece of paper should be labeled baking soda and the cups marked *#3* and *#4*. The rest of each sheet of paper can be used to record observations. Ask the students if they know what baking powder and baking soda are used for.

2. Have the students put one teaspoon of baking powder in cups #1 and #2 and, using a clean spoon, put one teaspoon of baking soda in cups #3 and #4. Stop there and ask them to suggest why there are two cups of each kind. Why did they need to use a clean spoon? What do they think they will do next?

3. Starting with the baking powder cups, have the students add two tablespoons of water to cup #1 and two tablespoons of vinegar to cup #2. What happens? Have them write their observations on the paper on which the cups are placed.

4. Using the second tablespoon, the students will do the same with cups #3 and #4. Again they will observe and write down their observations.

Analysis • On the board write *#1, #2, #3,* and *#4*. Have the students share their observations of each. What caused the foam in cups #1, #2, and #4? How were the results with cup #3 different from the others?

Application • The simple cake recipe on the application sheet can be made by the students at home or at school (if an oven is available). Have them observe and report back what happens when they add the vinegar to the mixture. Did the cake get higher while it was baking? What caused that?

Explanation • Both baking powder and baking soda are used in baking cakes and some breads. They produce bubbles of carbon dioxide gas, which push the cake or bread batter up. Baking powder is a mixture of sodium bicarbonate, an acid, and other materials. Baking soda is only sodium bicarbonate, with no acid added. Sodium bicarbonate plus an acid will produce bubbles of carbon dioxide gas. The baking powder already contained an acid, so it produced bubbles when water was added. The baking soda did not produce bubbles when water was added. It needed an acid, vinegar, to produce the bubbles.

• FIZZ!! •

You can make this cake at home. As you make it, make notes about what happens. Look, listen, and smell. Does anything happen when you mix the dry ingredients (the flour, sugar, cocoa, baking soda and salt) together? What happens when you add the vinegar? Why? How does the cake look before you bake it? Is it a solid or a liquid? Before you put the cake in the oven, measure how far the mixture is from the top of the pan. After you bake it, measure it again. Has it changed? What happened? Is it a liquid or a solid?

Easy Chocolate Cake

You will need a cake pan that is 9 inches square. You will also need a measuring cup, a teaspoon, and a tablespoon. Before you start, set the oven to 350 degrees.

Ingredients

1 $\frac{1}{2}$ cups flour	5 tablespoons cooking oil
3 tablespoons cocoa	1 tablespoon vinegar
1 teaspoon baking soda	1 teaspoon vanilla
1 cup sugar	1 cup cold water
$\frac{1}{2}$ teaspoon salt	

1. Put the dry ingredients (flour, cocoa, baking soda, sugar, and salt) in the baking pan and mix them together.

2. Pour the liquids (oil, vinegar, vanilla, and water) over the top. What happened when you poured the vinegar in?

3. Mix everything together until all the dry ingredients are wet and are the same color. Be sure to check the corners of the pan. Notice how high the mixture is in the pan. You may want to measure it from the top of the pan to the cake mixture.

4. Put it in the oven and bake it for 30 minutes. You can tell if it is done by poking the middle of the cake with a toothpick. If the toothpick comes out clean, the cake is done. Let the cake cool.

5. Measure how high the cake is in the pan. What else changed?

APPLICATION SHEET

57. A PIECE OF MILK

Topic • Colloids

Materials • For each group of students: a small jar or clear plastic cup, approximately one half cup of <u>whole</u> milk (note: this will not work with low fat or skim milk), one tablespoon of vinegar, a spoon, a piece of writing paper; if possible, a flashlight and a watch or clock with a second hand or digital seconds indicator. For each student: a copy of the A Piece of Milk Application Sheet.

Demonstration

1. Have the students describe the milk (color, taste, smell). Is it a liquid or a solid? Have them look at it with the flashlight.

2. Each group will need a reporter and a timekeeper. First have the reporter write the word *predictions* on the paper. Ask the students, working in their groups, to predict what will happen when they add the vinegar to the milk. Will the milk be different? The reporter should record the predictions. On the same paper, the reporter should write the words *10 seconds, 1 minute, 2 minutes, 3 minutes, 4 minutes,* and *5 minutes,* with a space after each one for recording observations at those intervals.

3. Tell the students to stir the vinegar into the milk and to observe the mixture carefully, using a flashlight if possible. As the timekeeper announces the passing of each time interval, have the reporter write down the students' observations at each one.

Analysis • Have each reporter tell the group's observations to the class. Did every group get the same result? What was it? Was the milk a solid or a liquid?

Application • Ask the students to read the story on the application sheet. Have them discuss what Maria might tell the teacher. Should Maria tell the teacher she disagrees with him?

Explanation • Milk is a mixture of liquids and tiny solid pieces. The solid pieces are spread throughout the liquid. This kind of mixture is called a *colloid*. When you add vinegar to milk, the small solid pieces clump together and form larger solid pieces. The remaining liquid is clear.

• A PIECE OF MILK •

Maria was in her ESL class. Her teacher was talking about ways to count objects in English. The teacher said, "In English you can say 'one car' or 'one man,' but not 'one water' or 'one bread.' You have to say 'a cup of water' or 'a piece of bread.'"

Maria thought about this and raised her hand. "What about 'a piece of milk'?" she asked. "Oh, no," her teacher said. "Milk is a liquid. You can say 'a glass of milk' or 'a cup of milk' or even 'a gallon of milk,' but you can't say 'a piece of milk.'"

1. Who is right? Explain why.

2. What would you tell the teacher if you were Maria?

58. ACID OR BASE?

Topic • Acid/base indicator

Materials • A large jar of red cabbage water (water in which you have cooked red cabbage; you may want to bring a leaf or two to class so the students know what you used), vinegar (acid), lemon juice (acid), baking soda (base); for each group: a small plastic cup and spoon, a copy of the Acid or Base? Student Sheet. For the Application: purple grape juice (acid), baking soda, water, a cup, a cotton swab or toothpick, a sheet of white paper.

Demonstration • (Note: You might want to start with the Application in order to arouse the students' curiosity.)

1. Pass around the jar of red cabbage water to see if the students can identify it. Show them the leaves. Explain that they are going to use this water to test some chemicals and find out more about them. Pass around the vinegar, lemon juice, and baking soda. Ask the students to tell you what they know about them: how they taste, what they are used for, etc.

2. Divide the students into small groups. Give each group a plastic cup with a small amount of the cabbage water in it. Then tell the students to follow the directions on the student sheet.

Analysis • Review the students' observations recorded in the Analysis section of the student sheet. Ask them to discuss the final question: *What did you observe?*

Application • Have the students write secret messages. In a cup, dissolve one tablespoon of baking soda in one tablespoon of water. This is the invisible ink. Have the students dip a cotton swab or a toothpick in the solution and write a message to a classmate on a sheet of white paper. Let the words dry completely, so the paper looks blank.

    Distribute the secret messages. Have each student dip a cotton swab in purple grape juice and rub it over the paper. The message will appear in blue-green letters. The baking soda is a base and the grape juice acts as an indicator, just as the cabbage juice did.

(Note: You may want to use this as an introduction to this lesson. Use the indicator solution to write short messages to the students conveying information related to classwork. When they ask how you did it, begin the demonstration).

Explanation • Some chemicals, such as vinegar and lemon juice, are called **acids**. Acids usually taste sour (if you can drink them) and are **corrosive**, that is, they eat away at other materials. Some other chemicals are called **bases**. Bases taste bitter and often feel slippery. The demonstration you just did showed a way of finding out if a material is an acid or a base. The red cabbage juice acted as an **indicator**, a chemical that changes color for acids and bases. When you added a base, the baking soda, it turned a greenish-blue. When you added an acid, lemon juice or vinegar, it turned red.

Follow-up • Make indicator strips by cutting blotting paper or heavy construction paper into strips and dipping them in the cabbage water. Let them dry. Have the students take them home and test materials they find there, such as orange juice, tomatoes, apples, or milk, and report back to the class.

• ACID OR BASE? •

Directions

1. Add a spoonful of baking soda to the red cabbage water. What happens? Record the results in the Analysis section, below, on the line following Step 1.

2. Add a spoonful of lemon juice to the water. What happens? Record the results for Step 2.

3. Add another spoonful of baking soda. Record the results for Step 3.

4. Add a spoonful of vinegar. Record the results for Step 4.

Analysis

Step 1: _____

Step 2: _____

Step 3: _____

Step 4: _____

What did you observe?

59. ROOM FOR MORE

Topic • Molecules

Materials • A transparent plastic container (with about one pint capacity), marbles, sand, a pitcher of water, a sponge or paper towel, a tea-spoon, a container of salt, a clear drinking glass, a plate.

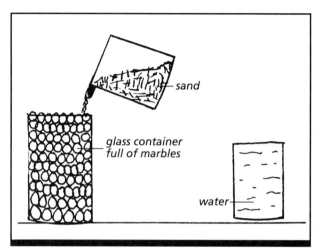

sand

glass container full of marbles

water

Demonstration

1. Fill the transparent container to the brim with marbles. Ask the students to describe what they see. Have a volunteer try to add more marbles to the container. Can the container hold any more marbles? Is it full?

2. Ask a volunteer to add sand to the container of marbles. Shake the container to settle the sand in between the marbles. Is the container full? Can anything else be added?

3. Now have a volunteer add water to the container. Was it possible to add water to the already full container? Can anything else be added?

Analysis • Ask the students to try to explain how the container, which was full of marbles, could hold sand. How could the container which was full of marbles and sand hold water? Would it be possible to start with a full container of water and add marbles and sand? Why not? Could other materials be used in this demonstration?

Application • (Note: This activity can be done as a demonstration for the whole class or by groups.) Fill a glass to the top with water. Continue to add water until it begins to run over the edge. Use a sponge to clean up the excess water. Does everyone agree that

the container is full? Show the students the salt. Ask if they think there is room for some salt in the water. Have a volunteer fill the measuring spoon with salt and add it to the water. Have an observer check to see if any water ran over the top. Ask another student to stand at the chalkboard and keep track of how much salt you add to the water. Add and record the amount of salt until the water runs over the top. (It should take two to three teaspoons.)

Explanation • The marbles, sand, and water were used as a model of how molecules of different sizes behave. The smaller sized molecules can slip in between the larger ones. The grains of sand fit into the spaces between the marbles and the water fit in between the marbles and the sand. When you added salt to the water it did not take up any more room than the water itself. That is because there are small empty pockets around the water molecules. The tiny molecules of the salt fit into the spaces between the water molecules and do not take up extra space. When those spaces are filled up, the water begins to run over the edge of the glass.

Heat

60. CUPS

Topic • Conduction

Materials • Two thermometers (borrowed from the science laboratory), a Styrofoam cup, a ceramic cup, hot water in a thermos.

Demonstration

1. Show the students the thermos. Have them tell you what they know about such containers. Ask them to guess what is inside it. Show them the cups and ask them to describe them and tell some differences between them. Finally, show them the thermometers and ask them to tell you what they know about them.

2. Have a student volunteer pour some water from the thermos into each cup and put a thermometer in it. Ask another student to read the temperature on each thermometer. Record the temperature and the time on the board. Ask the students to guess about the next reading. Do they think the water temperature in both cups will be the same? Why or why not?

3. After one minute, record the time and the temperature again. Were the students' guesses right? How much did the temperature change in each cup? Have several student volunteers feel the outsides of the cups. Do they seem to be the same temperature?

4. After another minute, record the time and temperature again. What can the students conclude from their observations?

Analysis • As a class, make a chart on the board showing how the temperatures changed. Calculate the changes in temperature in each cup as well as the differences between them.

Application • Divide the class into groups of three or four students. Tell each group to try to invent a way to keep a jar of hot water hot for a long time. What could you put around the jar? Have each group share its ideas. Try out the ones you think would work best (and which are feasible).

Explanation • When you began the experiment, the water temperature in both cups was the same. As you continued to measure temperatures, the temperature in the ceramic cup dropped

faster than the temperature in the foam cup. At the same time, the ceramic cup became warmer, while the foam cup did not show much change in temperature. The heat from the water in the ceramic cup traveled through the material of the cup, making the cup hotter. This is called **conduction**. If you put a metal spoon in a cup of hot water, it gets hot very quickly. This is because metal is a good **conductor**. The ceramic cup is not as good a conductor as a metal spoon, but it is a better conductor than the foam cup. Materials that do not conduct heat well are called **insulators**.

61. BUTTER MELTDOWN

Topic • Conduction

Materials • Three spoons of approximately the same size: one made of wood (a tongue depressor can be substituted), one of plastic, and one of metal; a container in which the spoons can stand up; boiling water in a thermos; three small pats of butter; three dried beans

Demonstration

1. Attach a bean to the handle end of each spoon with a pat of butter. Make the distance from the other end of the spoon to the bean the same for all three.

2. Lean the spoons against the edge of the container. They should all be at the same angle.

3. Carefully add the boiling water to the container.

4. Have the students predict what will happen. Ask questions such as: *Will the beans stay on the spoons? If they fall off, which one will fall off first? Why?*

Analysis • Have the students 1) tell what happened and 2) try to explain why one bean fell off before the others.

Application • Divide the students into groups and ask them to think about hot objects with which they come in contact. Which objects used some sort of insulating material to protect the user and which did not? Have them divide the objects into two groups on that basis and to describe the insulating material for the first group. Each group of students can present their findings to the class.

Explanation • Heat is transferred through objects by a process called **conduction**. Conduction is heat movement. When the molecules of a metal object are heated, they begin to vibrate. As the molecules move and bump into adjacent molecules, they also move. As they move, they create heat. Little by little, all the molecules are in motion and the object becomes hot.

Some materials conduct heat well and some do not. In good

conductors, such as most metals, the molecules are free to move around easily and so can hit each other and make heat; but in poor conductors the molecules cannot move around easily and so it is difficult for them to transfer heat. In this experiment, metal is a good conductor, so the heat passes quickly through the metal spoon and melts the butter; but wood and plastic are poor conductors, and so the heat does not pass through them easily to melt the butter. Poor conductors are called **insulators**.

62. BLOW UP

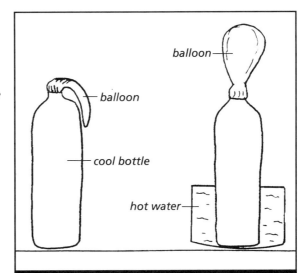

balloon

balloon

cool bottle

hot water

Topic • Expansion

Materials • Two identical empty plastic bottles without caps, a balloon, a bowl, hot water, ice cubes; access to a nearby refrigerator is necessary.

Demonstration

1. Chill one of the plastic bottles in the refrigerator until just before the demonstration. Pass around the other empty bottle and ask the students to describe it. What does it look like? What's inside it? Show the students the balloon. Ask them to tell what happens when a person blows into a balloon. Introduce the word **expand**. Tell them that you are going to use the air inside the bottle to make the balloon expand. Ask the students if they think it is possible. How could that happen?

2. Get out the chilled bottle and have a student volunteer fit the balloon over the top. Have the volunteer identify any way(s) that the bottle is different from the one they have already looked at.

3. Pour the hot water in the bowl and put the bottle inside it. Have the students observe what happens to the balloon. What made the balloon expand?

4. Add ice to the water in the bowl. What happens to the balloon? Why?

Analysis • Divide the students into small groups. Have the students make a list of things they have seen expand when they are hot and contract when they are cold. Are there any materials that expand when they are cold? (Water is different from other materials in that it expands when it freezes.)

Application • Write the following problem on the board and have the students read it, or ask them to listen as you read it. Then have them work in small groups to brainstorm solutions.

In a certain city there is a big building project. They are building an enormous arch, which will be 630 feet high when it is finished. It is made of stainless steel. The builders start by building each leg of the arch. Finally they are ready to put in the keystone, the center piece at the top of the arch. It is a very hot summer day. The builders find that there is not enough space for the keystone because the steel has expanded in the heat. What can they do to solve this problem?

After the students have worked on the problem, have them share their solutions. You may then want to share the following information with them, either orally or in writing.

The Gateway Arch is part of the Jefferson National Expansion Memorial in St. Louis, Missouri. It represents the expansion to the West of the United States. It was designed by the Finnish-born architect Eero Saarinen and is 630 feet (192 meters) high. When it was being completed in the summer of 1964, the heat had expanded the stainless steel so that the workers were unable to put in the keystone. They asked the fire department for help. The firefighters sprayed water on the legs of the Arch to make it cooler. The workers were then able to put in the keystone.

Explanation • When you put the hot water in the bowl, you heated the bottle and the air inside it. As the air became hotter, it **expanded**. It took up more space than it did before. Most materials become slightly larger when they are heated and slightly smaller when they are cooled. All materials are made up of atoms and molecules. The atoms and molecules move all the time. As they move, they hit each other. As they get hotter, they move faster and hit each other harder. As a result, they occupy more space. The reverse is true when materials become cooler. There are examples of expansion and contraction all around you, such as thermometers and thermostats. Builders leave gaps in bridges and sidewalks to allow for expansion.

63. POP!!

Topic • Expansion

Materials • Unpopped popcorn, a hot-air popcorn popper, ruler with ¹/₁₆ inch (or 1 mm) divisions

Demonstration

1. Show the students the unpopped corn in a bowl. Write the word *popcorn* on the board, and ask them to describe popcorn, telling how it feels, smells, and looks. Record their observations on the board or on a large piece of paper. Have someone measure a few kernels. Record the measurements. In a measuring cup, measure the amount you are going to pop. If you have an appropriate scale, you might weigh the corn before popping it. Students may want to compare names for popcorn in their first languages and associations they make with it. You may want to share some American associations: movie theaters, popcorn balls or popcorn strings, cozy family times.

2. Pop the corn in the popper.

3. Have students describe, measure, and weigh the popcorn after popping. Record the results next to the previous observations.

Analysis • Compare the "before" and "after" observations. Ask the students to tell or write statements comparing the corn before and after popping. What caused the changes?

Application • Divide the students into groups. Ask each group to brainstorm and write down as many possible uses of popcorn as they can. (These might range from food to pillow stuffing.) Offer a prize to the group that can come up with (and explain) the most uses. Set a time limit of 10 or 15 minutes on the brainstorming. Then have each group present and explain its ideas.

Explanation • Before the corn is popped, each piece, or *kernel*, has a hard shell on the outside. Inside the kernel is a material called *starch* and a little water. When the kernel gets hot, the water evaporates, that is, it turns into a gas. When that happens, it pushes on the outer shell and breaks it. This blows the starch that is inside to the outside.

64. HOT HANGER

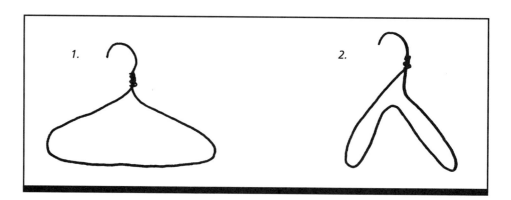

Topic • Friction

Materials • A wire coat hanger for each group of two to four students. (Alternately, a 9-inch piece of wire of the same thickness can be used.)

Demonstration

1. Begin the experiment by asking the class how they warm their hands when they are cold. Someone will probably suggest rubbing them together. Have the students rub their hands together. What happens? Does anyone have any idea why their hands get warmer? You may want to introduce the word **friction**. (If your students have done Lesson 18, Slides, and Lesson 19, Rollers, have them tell what they learned about friction.)

2. Show the students the coat hangers. Ask them to tell you about the coat hangers. What are they made of? What are some uses for them? Tell them that they are going to heat up a hanger without using a flame. Ask if anyone has any ideas about how they will do it.

3. Divide the students into groups and give each group a hanger. Tell them to feel the coat hanger all over. How does it feel? Smooth? Cool?

4. Now tell each group to choose one person to do the experiment. The rest of the group will be observers. Have the experimenter bend the hanger in half once. Tell the observers to

feel the hanger again, then instruct the experimenter to bend and unbend the hanger ten times quickly. Now have the observers touch the bent part of the hanger.

Analysis • Have the students in their groups try to explain the relationship between rubbing their hands together and the hot hanger.

Application • Present this material to your students orally or in writing:

Most of you have used a microwave oven. What are some ways that cooking in a microwave is different from cooking with a stove? Probably the first thing you notice is how fast a microwave oven cooks. You can bake a potato in a microwave in about three minutes, but in an oven it takes an hour to bake a potato. The other thing you may have observed is that the food you put in the microwave gets hot, but its container does not. Both of these things occur because microwave ovens cook things in a special way.

When you turn on a microwave, a part of the oven called the magnetron *sends out short waves (microwaves). These waves bounce off of metal (such as the walls of the oven) and go right through glass, plastic, or paper containers to the food that is in them. Inside the food, these waves cause the molecules to vibrate quickly and rub against each other. This friction creates heat, just as the friction of rubbing your hands together or bending the hanger created heat.*

Explanation • When you bent the hanger back and forth quickly, the hanger got hot. In the same way, when you rub your hands together, they feel warmer. In both cases you created friction. When you rubbed your hands together, there was friction between them. Some of the energy from this friction takes the form of heat. When you bent the hanger, you didn't have two separate objects rubbing together, but you had the molecules within the hanger rubbing. Again, this resulted in heat being given off.

65. HOT OR COLD?

Topic • Perception

Materials • A bowl filled with ice water, a bowl filled with hot tap water, a bowl filled with lukewarm water.

Demonstration

1. Put the bowl of lukewarm water between the other two bowls.

2. Ask a student to place one hand in the hot water and the other hand in the ice water for two minutes. While she is doing this ask the other students to predict what is going to happen next.

3. Then ask the student to place both hands in the lukewarm water and to report how her hands feel.

4. Allow several other volunteers to repeat the activity.

Analysis • In groups, have students try to explain why the lukewarm water feels hot to one hand but cold to the other. Then ask them to share their explanations with other groups.

Application • Ask your students to answer the following questions in pairs: *Would you rather jump into a swimming pool after a hot shower or a cold shower? Why? Does the pool feel cooler when you first get in or later? Why?*

Explanation • Nerve endings in your hand send messages to your brain about how hot or cold the water is. After a while, these nerve endings get used to the temperature of the water they are in, whether it is hot or cold. When you suddenly put them in the lukewarm water, they feel that the water is hot or cold in comparison with the temperature of the water they were just in.

66. HOT COLORS

Topic • Reflection/absorption

Materials • One white sock and one black sock for each group. The socks should be identical except for color. If possible, do this activity outdoors on a sunny day. If that is not possible, bring in a few small lamps with 100 watt light bulbs.

Demonstration

1. Take the class outdoors. Have the students look at objects around them. Which ones do they think will feel hot? Which will feel cold? Have students touch some of the surfaces to see whether or not they are right. Why do they think some are hot and others are cool?

2. Divide the class into small groups. Give each group one black sock and one white sock.

3. Tell one person from each group to begin by putting the black sock on one hand and the white sock on the other. After a few minutes of exposure to the sun or the lamp, which hand feels warmer? Have the group members take turns doing the demonstration.

Analysis • Which colors would you choose to wear in hot weather? In cold weather? Why do people in hot countries often paint their houses white? What are some other examples of people using white or light colors to reflect heat and dark colors to absorb it?

Application • Find the following locations on a map: Alaska, Arizona, Norway, and Saudi Arabia. If you have done Lesson 26, Make a Compass, have them describe the location of each place in relation to its neighbors. What do the students know about each place? Have each student choose one of the places and draw and color a picture of clothing, a house, and a car with colors that would be suitable for that place. Have them share their pictures and explain their choices.

Explanation • As you saw in the demonstration, the hand that had the black sock on it got hotter than the one with the white sock on it. This is because the color black **absorbs** heat from the sun. Dull and dark surfaces absorb more heat than shiny and light surfaces do. Shiny and light surfaces **reflect** some of the radiation and do not become as hot.

APPENDICES

TABLE I

Correlation of Common ESL Themes with Eureka! Lessons

Common ESL Themes	Lessons
Animals	3. Outdoor Scavenger Hunt, page 7
	4. Animal Tracks, page 10
	35. A Hole in the Hand, page 101
	36. The Bird in the Cage, page 103
	38. We're All Ears, page 110
	49. Will It or Won't It? page 135
Body	15. Balancing Acts, page 46
	30. After the Bell, page 89
	31. Lenses, page 92
	34. Liquid Light, page 99
	35. A Hole in the Hand, page 101
	36. The Bird in the Cage, page 103
	37. Where's the Sound? page 107
	38. We're All Ears, page 110
	39. Coat Hanger Chimes, page 111
	41. Scratching the Surface, page 116
	42. Echo... Echo... Echo... page 118
	43. Drum Beat, page 120
	49. Will It or Won't It? page 135
Colors	30. After the Bell, page 89
	32. Colored Water/Colored Air, page 94
	50. Floating Colors, page 137
	55. What Color Is It? page 152
	58. Acid or Base? page 159
	66. Hot Colors, page 177
Communication	29. Now You Hear It, Now You Don't, page 84
	40. Canned Messages, page 113
Directions, Map Reading	9. The Underwater Paper Mystery, page 29
	10. The Upside Down Glass of Water, page 32
	17. Wrong Way? page 52

TABLE 2

Correlation of Demonstration Steps with Grammatical/Structural Items

Section	Language likely to be generated	Possible language activities (elaborated in the text)

Picture	imperatives
	prepositions
	descriptors
	there is/there are
	question forms
	future tense
	conditionals
	vocabulary for the
	  specific lesson
		1. predict what the
		   demonstration is about
		2. label the picture
		3. describe and draw
		4. retell and draw
		5. write a description

Materials	imperatives
	prepositions
	question forms
	future tense
	modals (*might, could be,*
	  can't be, etc.)
	descriptors
	vocabulary for the
	  specific lesson
		1. guess the mystery
		2. name and describe
		   objects
		3. brainstorm uses
		4. predict what the
		   demonstration will be

Demonstration	imperatives prepositions question forms clarifying information	1. listen to (or read) and follow directions 2. team dictation

Analysis	past tense
	conditionals
	comparatives
	agreement and
	  disagreement
	suggesting
	reporting
	describing
		1. channel conversion
		2. retelling
		3. language experience
		   work with retelling
		4. problem solving

Section	Language likely to be generated	Possible language activities (elaborated in the text)
Application	The Applications are, themselves, language activities, generating a variety of language forms.	
Explanation	cause and effect definitions sequence examples	1. student theorizing 2. oral explanation by teacher or student informant 3. written text as jigsaw cut up text, cloze, gradually revealed 4. partial dictation 5. rewrite text

LIST OF REPRODUCIBLES

The pages listed here may be reproduced for classroom use.

GLOSSARY

The following glossary is intended for the use of the teacher. It provides definitions and suggestions for explaining terms indicated in boldface type in the demonstrations as well as some more general terms. We have tried to keep the number of entries to a minimum. Many other terms are clearly and explicitly defined within individual demonstrations and are therefore not included here. We have used italics in the text to indicate words which should be pointed out and emphasized to students.

absorb: to take in, as with water, heat, and sound. A sponge is a good example of an object that can absorb.

acid: one of a large group of corrosive chemicals. Vinegar and lemon juice are common examples.

action: motion or movement.

adhesion: the property of sticking to another material. Cellophane tape and glue are both adhesive.

air pressure: a measure of how often the molecules in the air bump into each other in a given area.

antenna: the part of a radio system from which a signal is sent or at which it is received. Many students are familiar with antennas on a radio, TV set, or portable telephone.

balance: the point at which weight is evenly distributed. A good illustration of balance is to hold a small book or other object on one finger.

base: one of a large group of chemicals that neutralize or work against acids. Lye and washing soda are examples.

Bernoulli's Principle: pressure in a moving fluid decreases as the speed of the fluid increases. This applies to air as well as to liquids.

Celsius: a system for measuring temperatures in which the boiling point of water is 100° and the freezing point of water is O°. To convert Celsius to Fahrenheit, multiply the Celsius temperature by 9, divide the answer by 5, and add 32. Also called **centigrade**.

center of gravity: that point in an object or person around which its weight is evenly balanced.

cohesion: the mutual attraction that holds the elements of a body together.

conduction: the transfer of heat energy by direct contact between particles.

conductor: a substance that allows either electricity or heat to flow through it easily. Copper is a good example of a conductor.

corrosive: a chemical that can eat away metal.

degrees: units of measurement for temperatures. Celsius and Fahrenheit are both systems for measuring temperatures.

density: how heavy an object is in relation to its size. To demonstrate density, put both a cork and a nail in some water. Even though the cork is bigger than the nail, it will float, but the nail will not. That is because the cork weighs less in proportion to its size than the nail does.

displacement: the weight or volume of a fluid displaced by a floating body. To illustrate displacement, mark the water level in a plastic cup. Then drop an object in it and observe where the new water level is.

dissolve: To make a solid combine with a liquid. Molecules of a solid material (the solute) spread out evenly among the molecules of a liquid (the solvent). The particles are not visible and will not settle out.

electromagnet: a coil of wire wound around an iron core. It becomes a magnet only when electrical current runs through the wire.

expand: to swell out or increase in size, often as a result of being heated.

Fahrenheit: a system for measuring temperatures. At 32 degrees Fahrenheit, water freezes; at 212 degrees Fahrenheit, water boils. To convert Fahrenheit to Celsius, subtract 32 from the Fahrenheit temperature, multiply by 5, and divide the answer by 9.

force: a push or pull.

freezing point: the temperature at which a liquid turns into a solid. In the case of water, the freezing point is 32° F or 0° C.

friction: the rubbing of one object against another. Friction slows down the movement of objects and creates heat. A common example is the brakes on a bicycle or rubber-soled shoes on a floor.

gravity: the force that tends to draw all bodies toward the center of the earth. To demonstrate gravity, drop a pencil or other object on the floor and observe whether it went up or down.

indicator: a substance that changes color in the presence of an acid or base.

inertia: the tendency of an object to remain at rest if it is at rest and to remain in motion if it is moving, unless it is affected by an outside force. To demonstrate inertia, use a marble or similar small, round object. First put it at rest on a flat surface. Observe whether it will move by itself. Then push it and observe whether it will continue moving by itself.

insulator: a substance that does not allow electricity or heat to pass through it easily.

lens: a piece of curved, transparent material that focuses light. A good example is a magnifying glass.

lever: a simple machine that consists of a bar that turns or pivots around a fixed point.

lift: the force of upward motion.

liquid: the state of matter that has a definite volume but not a definite shape.

magnet: a material that produces a magnetic force which attracts iron, cobalt, or nickel.

magnetic field: the space around a magnet in which its magnetic force works.

melting point: the temperature at which a solid becomes a liquid. In the case of water, this is 32° F or 0° C.

molecule: a particle that contains two or more atoms joined together.

motion: the change in position of an object as compared with a reference point.

negative charge: an object with a negative electrical charge has more electrons than protons.

Newton's Laws of Motion: 1. An object at rest remains at rest until a force acts on it. An object in motion remains in motion until a force acts upon it. 2. The greater the mass, the greater the force needed to move it. 3. For every action there is an opposite and equal reaction.

optical illusion: a misleading visual image; something you think you see.

optics: the scientific study of light and vision

positive charge: an object with a positive electrical charge has more protons than electrons.

pressure: force exerted on an opposing body. To demonstrate pressure, press on the back of a student's hand; have that person press on another's, etc.

radio waves: a form of radiant energy used in communications and broadcasting.

reaction: in physics: the equal and opposite response to an action; in chemistry: the result of mixing two or more substances together.

reflection: the bouncing back of heat, light, and sound, for example, the reflection of light rays from a mirror.

refraction: the bending of light when it goes from one material to another.

solid: the state of matter that has a definite shape and a definite volume.

solution: the result of adding a material to a liquid, in which the particles are spread evenly throughout the liquid, are not visible, and do not settle out.

static electricity: electricity in the form of charged particles, either positive or negative. These stay in the object and do not flow like electrical current.

surface tension: the cohesive force on the outer surface of a liquid.

temperature: the measure of how hot or cold something is.

vacuum: a completely empty space, with no solids, liquids, or gases in it.

velocity: speed in a definite direction.

vibration: rapid, rhythmic motion back and forth. To demonstrate vibration, use a rubber band. Have one student hold it taut between his fingers and have another pluck it, like a guitar string.

weight: the amount of gravitational pull on an object.

work: using force to move an object.

RESOURCES

The following is a short list of books which are useful for teaching science to ESL students. Most are inexpensive paperbacks available at local bookstores.

Amery, Heather and Angela Littler. *The KnowHow Book of Batteries and Magnets*. London: Usborne Publishing, 1975.

Cash, Terry, Steve Parker, and Barbara Taylor. *175 More Science Experiments to Amuse and Amaze Your Friends*. New York: Random House, 1991.

Church, Jok. *You Can With Beakman: Science Stuff You Can Do*. Kansas City: Andrews and McMeel, 1992.

Craig, Annabel and Cliff Rosney. *The Usborne Science Encyclopedia*. London: Usborne Publishing, 1988.

Edom, Helen. *Science with Magnets*. London: Usborne Publishing Company, 1992.

Gold, Carol. *Science Express: 50 Scientific Stunts from the Ontario Science Center*. Reading: Addison-Wesley, 1991.

Hart-Davis, Adam. *Scientific Eye*. New York: Sterling Publishing, 1989.

Johnson, Mary. *Pocket Scientist Chemistry Experiments*. London: Usborne Publishing, 1981.

Kent, Amanda and Alan Ward. *Introduction to Physics*. London: Usborne Publishing, 1983.

Ladizinsky, Eric. *Magical Science: Magic Tricks for Young Scientists*. Los Angeles: Lowell House Juvenile, 1992.

Liem, Tik L. *Invitations to Science Inquiry*. Science Inquiry Enterprises, 14358 Village View Lane, Chino Hills, California 91709.

Macaulay, David. *The Way Things Work*. Boston: Houghton Mifflin, 1988.

Melton, Lisa and Eric Ladizinsky. *Fifty Nifty Science Experiments*. Los Angeles: Lowell House Juvenile, 1992.

Oxlade, Chris, Corinne Stockley and Jane Wertheim. *The Usborne Illustrated Dictionary of Physics*. London: Usborne Publishing, 1988.

——. *The Usborne Illustrated Dictionary of Science.* London: Usborne Publishing, 1988.

VanCleave, Janice Pratt. *Janice VanCleave's Chemistry for Every Kid: 101 Easy Experiments that Really Work.* New York: John Wiley and Sons, 1989.

——. *Janice VanCleave's Physics for Every Kid: 101 Easy Experiments in Motion, Heat, Light, Machines and Sound.* New York: John Wiley and Sons, 1991.

——. *Janice Van Cleave's Molecules: Spectacular Science Projects.* New York: John Wiley and Sons, 1993.

Walpole, Brenda. *175 Science Experiments to Amuse and Amaze Your Friends.* New York: Random House, 1988.

Wonder Science. American Chemical Association, 1155 16th St., NW, Washington, D.C. 20036. (published periodically)

Wood, Jenny. *Storms.* Richmond Hill: Scholastic Canada, 1990.